# Discipline Strategies
## For The Bored,
## Belligerent and Ballistic
## In Your Classroom

### A Survival Guide For Teachers

—————≻•◖◖◖◖◗◗◗•≺—————

## Carol Fuery

21321

# Acknowledgments

To Chelle Koster Walton, Rosie Wysong and George Ruot for their sensitive and encouraging editing.

To Kelly Madden for designing the cover and illustrations.

To Mary Harrell-Sesniak, Computer Services and Training, for layout design.

To Tawnya Whitaker for making copy changes and creating the back cover.

To Barbara Ward, Principal Sanibel Elementary School for her suggestions.

To all the teachers and administrators I have met in seminars across this country, your stories and comments made this book possible.

Sanibel SandDollar Publications, Inc.
P.O. Box 461, Captiva, FL 33924
800-330-3459 Fax: 941-472-0699

# Contents

## Appendix

To Order Books

# **Dedication**

I dedicate this book to my mother, Pauline Cartee Bailey, and to my father, James C. Bailey, Sr., who taught me the art of self-discipline.

I also dedicate this book to my darling husband, George Robert Ruot, who shares my Sanibel Island sunsets and creates the hopes that follow love.

# 1

## *Meet Bored, Ballistic Billy*

**B**illy Carleton, a seventh grader, is thrown out of your middle school classroom. He burped loudly, leaned back in his chair and punched the boy behind him. It's the fifth time in two weeks.

Billy sprawls in one of the straight chairs lining the closed office door. Mr. Etheridge, the assistant principal, emerges. He asks, "Why are you here?" The answer is always, "I don't know."

"What'd you do this time?"

"I didn't do nothing."

Eventually a confession will take place. Billy will promise to be good for the rest of the period, for the rest of the day, for the remainder of his life, whatever it takes. He's an expert.

### The Hero Returns

Less than 15 minutes later, Billy strolls into class, a veteran home on holiday from the war. He's cocky, confident, bears a pink copy of the referral slip in his hand. He announces, "He didn't do nothing."

And Belligerent Billy is right.

You want to strangle him. You'd even derive great pleasure from strangling Mr. Etheridge. It's a short-term solution headed for long-term disaster.

Every time you send a student to the office, you lose. It is a "wait 'til your father comes home and he'll give you a whipping" mentality. Unresolved discipline problems aren't self-healing wounds. Left unattended, they get worse. Teachers feel defeated, dejected and discouraged.

They aren't the only ones. An assistant principal told me, "I'm very frustrated. I feel like I'm putting out small fires. I'm not solving problems in the long run." He is right.

When we excuse Billy's behavior, we do him, as well as other students, a disservice. We tell them in subtle ways that they don't have what it takes to be good and to be smart, so they're excused from trying.

## Dysfunctional Families

"Ozzie and Harriet" and "Father Knows Best" were ideal fantasies. We didn't have families like that when we were growing up, and the students today don't have ideal families either. Destructive young people use their parents, their age, their poverty and their peers as excuses for being out of control. These excuses aren't acceptable.

## What Is Discipline?

Discipline is a basic set of rules needed to resolve problems and accomplish goals. These rules enable students to experience problems, work through them, and learn and grow in the process. Discipline brings lives under control.

"Perhaps the most valuable results of all education is the ability to make yourself do the thing you have to do when it ought to be done, whether you like it or not; it is the first lesson that ought to be learned; and however early a man's training begins, it is probably the last lesson that he learns thoroughly."

Thomas Huxley, English author

Doing what needs to be done means making a commitment. Good classroom discipline begins with commitment and responsibility. I'm in charge of the discipline, not an assistant principal or dean. I set the limits. And if I'm not self-disciplined, then directing the lives of students lacks integrity.

## Discipline Is An Art

We can't discipline all students in the same way. I ask myself, "How can I get this child to respond most favorably? What works best? Could it be story-telling, increased positive attention, a planned confrontation?"

If I wish to be heard, I need to speak at the listener's level and in a language he/she can understand.

## Are You Kid Smart?

Kid smart is street wise. It's back alley savvy. Those who aren't savvy become bored and belligerent teachers. They languish in repetitious teaching jobs; they say they feel hollow, empty and unfulfilled. They're stuck, refusing to grow where they're planted.

They blame principals, colleagues and their families for their unhappiness. Ironically, with all their years of experience, many of these teachers are quite perceptive, even intuitive. Their instincts are merely dulled. What they pick up perceptively, they misuse.

Deep down they know what should and should not be said, when and when not to say it. They can't help themselves. They blurt out indiscretions. Even when they know expressing anger is in their own worst interest, they can't check it.

This career immaturity afflicts as many teachers in their 40's and 50's as it does those in their 20's and 30's.

## Resist Impulsive Behavior

When a conflict needs to be handled discreetly, how do you rank your discretion? When a humorous or conciliatory remark might take the heat from an exchange, how cooling was your impulsiveness? The next time you're ready to act impulsively in the classroom, how will you resist the urge? In most discipline struggles, teachers have the edge. For too long we've thought otherwise.

Take the edge. Kids say and do things that provide a wealth of insights.

Gather everything you know about your students' likes, wishes, interests, hopes and dreams. Use this information.

## Try Something New

Gary Player, the South African pro golfer, once said, "The harder I practice, the luckier I get."

The first time we try a new strategy, it's like a lab experiment. We may not get it right.

Don't be discouraged. Try again. Good luck comes from concentrated practice.

The skills, strategies and suggestions in this book will make you luckier. But you'll need to practice them on our special clients, our students.

## You're the Heart of the School

The center, the heart of the school is not the bureaucratic maze that weighs us down. It's one teacher and one class. Working with the raw materials, the untapped talent, we can succeed. The number one person in the classroom is still the teacher.

If the teacher is confident, controlled and kid smart, then he/she can manage, train, and bring out the best in all students. The teacher can bring out that *"giftedness"* all children possess. If the teacher is bored, kids will be too.

## Part of the Package

"People say they want to be happy and they say they want the Garden of Eden, but really they want conflict. If we were given peace, love and harmony on a plate, we'd want to cover it with ketchup."

Boy George, English rock star

In dealing with all relationships, resistance and conflict are part of the package. We're getting paid to work with conflict. Without it, teaching would be dull.

## No Simple Solutions

The pendulum of discipline has swung too far. Many of us want discipline to be easy, with step-by-step instructions. We refuse to trust our instincts. We follow some rigid code of rules that requires checks by a kid's name. The accounting system would confuse a CPA. Others follow the "one method for all" way of treating students. Obviously, it is not working.

When intimidation fails, we try to become the student's friend. The average youngster has no shortage of friends. Young people need strong, determined teachers who set limits and impose consequences.

We need to be more than the adult with the car keys; more than someone who begs in a saccharine voice, "Jimmy, stop chasing your team mate with that machete, o-kay?"

## Too Much Psycho

We've read too much psycho-babble. We're told a child who misbehaves isn't misbehaving. He needs nurturing or he has unresolved issues or unexpressed anger. We avoid putting the responsibility on the child and asking him to stop acting like a brat. That might crush his delicate self-esteem.

Children's self-esteem can't be irreparably damaged with a misplaced word. Children are fairly durable people who need to be taught respect and responsibility.

## Assuming Responsibility

Behavior and crime can't be fully traced back to biological, psychological and/or sociological factors.

According to Victor Frankl, author of *Man's Search For Meaning*, "Totally explaining one's crime would be tantamount to explaining away guilt and to seeing in him/her not a free and responsible human being but a machine to be repaired. Even criminals themselves abhor this treatment and prefer to be held responsible for their deeds."

In a speech at San Quentin, Frankl addressed the prisoners with, "You are a human being like me, you were free to commit a crime, to become guilty. Now you are responsible for overcoming guilt by rising above it, by growing, by changing for the better."

Kids need to be taught that they have choices. They have a free will. They're responsible for their behavior. That's why discipline is crucial.

## Kids Live in Reality

The President gathered around him 50 youngsters of elementary school age through late teens. In the East Room, they quizzed him about one problem: crime. The most compelling words came from Annie Nichol of Calistoga, California. Her sister, Polly Klass, was abducted from a bedroom slumber party and murdered.

With a stuffed animal at her side, Annie told the President, "I asked my mom, do you think I'm going to live to grow up? My sister didn't grow up. I just don't feel safe anymore, and I want America to be safe for children."

## Safe Havens

I want my classroom to be a safe haven, physically and psychologically. Teaching kids about responsibility and discipline creates safe havens. It also takes time. The same time it would take to go in another, less productive direction.

"It costs us about $1,500 a year to educate a child. It costs $4,000 to incarcerate one. Whether you pay now or pay later, sooner or later, you're going to pay."

Mary Futrell, noted educator

## Teach Now or Jail Later

Nathan McCall, in his book, *Makes Me Want To Holler*, said, "Most of what I hear in the way of proposed solutions from politicians has to do with punishment. It has to do with vengeance. It's part of the whole effort to give people a false sense of safety."

For every 17-year-old they lock up for the rest of his life, there's some young boy who's just turned 17. So if you haven't dealt with the mind set that caused the first 17-year-old to go wrong, you can bet on the next one doing the same.

"Looking down the road, all we've done is built more prisons and warehoused more people, and we haven't addressed the insanity."

Nathan McCall makes a good point.

## Take Action Now

We have to catch kids while they are still malleable and redeemable. Waiting until they reach 17 is too late. We have lots of work to do, worthwhile work. We are salvaging our futures as well as theirs. Let's turn things around. I'll show you how.

# 2

# *Marketable Classrooms*
# *From Day One*

**R**ight from the beginning, successful teachers must make classrooms salable to kids. The teacher is the marketer, the specialist in promoting and providing services to the purchaser, our students.

If something is marketable, it's fit to be offered for sale. Marketing is not the art of selling. It's creating conditions that convince the buyer to purchase a product or a service. Teachers create conditions that make kids decide to buy into the classroom.

Students come to us full of hope and promise. On that first day of school, students enter our classrooms with a willingness to be won over. It's a prime, teachable moment. And how do we best use this prime time slot? We bore kids to death by reading them the rules from a handbook or by giving them reams of paperwork. We talk too much.

There is a better way. By controlling our students' impressions of us, we control the salability of our product, our classroom. When that initial impression is favorable, it's easier to get students to cooperate. I'll show you in this chapter how to be a maverick and set the stage for improved discipline all year long.

# Appear Organized

The reality on that first day back is that schools can be chaotic. Prepare for confusion by meeting the following responsibilities.

## Five Teacher Responsibilities

1. Get students in the right room.
2. Get students seated facing you.
3. Get students working.
4. Take attendance quietly.
5. Impress unobtrusively.

## 1. Get students in right room

Post your name and room number outside of the door. Inside the classroom, have this same information on the chalkboard or overhead projector. Wear a name tag. Stand at the door. As students enter, check schedules. Early arriving students can act as ushers. Post a seating chart inside the room.

## 2. Have students face you

If students face one another while you give rules, most likely you'll get the rolling of eyes and facial expressions that indicate disapproval. Avoid this by having kids face you.

### 3. Get students working

Rather than say, "I expect you to work in here," get kids working. Suggested assignments include: filling out a general information sheet, listening to an age-appropriate story, copying schedules, having students break into two-person teams and introducing their partners to the class and/or doing a written activity that keeps students engaged.

### 4. Take attendance

Why mispronounce a child's name? Take attendance through the seating chart. On the student information sheet (on page 25) is the one essential question, "What name do you like to be called?" Check this name against the "formal" roll sheet and correct your records.

### 5. Impress unobtrusively

An organized teacher is impressive. That's why we prepare for confusion and plan extra activities.

A second way to impress students is through an act or gesture of random kindness (one that nobody would miss if it weren't made). Because it's unexpected, the gesture gets noticed. It can be as simple as answering a question with kindness or lending a pencil quickly, automatically, before being asked.

Making an impression demands subtlety and self-awareness. Smart teachers are cognizant of what they say, and how they say it.

# Car Rental Catastrophe

You had a four-hour delayed flight from Florida to Chicago. It's late and you're exhausted. You pick up your luggage and head for the rental car agency. You wait in a long line, get up to the counter and hand over your driver's license and credit card.

The man behind the counter has been working too long. He is grumpy. Frowning, he hands you a form to sign and no pen. You feel through your pockets and realize you don't have a pen either.

When you ask for one, you hear, "What, you don't have a pen? Well what did you expect? I can't afford to lend you one. You have to learn responsibility. You just get right back on that plane and find one. You left your map of the city on your desk at home? My, wasn't that a good place for it? How will you be able to use it if it's at home?"

Does this sound painfully familiar? We demean kids in language we'd never use with adults.

Self-awareness is the key. That opening day, we have subtle opportunities for impressing students positively.

# Manage With an Invisible Hand

Mark McCormick, author of *What They Don't Teach You At Harvard Business School*, writes about creating impressions when he recalls a lunch meeting with Ray Cave, managing editor of *Time* magazine.

When we reached the restaurant, Ray greeted the maitre d' with, 'Good to see you again.' The maitre d' perked right up and immediately led us to our table.

13

After he disappeared, I said to Ray, "I thought you told me you had never eaten here before."

"I haven't," he said. Ray Cave knew the power of making someone feel special. Make students feel special that first week.

## Help Kids Fit In

Back to school promotions, newspapers and television advertising convince kids what to wear to be "top of their class." The right sneakers and perfectly faded blue jeans are essential for peer acceptance. Parents and working teens spend a fortune to look like everyone else.

Why? Because students are desperately trying to meet core needs — fitting in and feeling accepted. Helping kids feel accepted in our classrooms is essential for our success in teaching them.

## Listen for the Truth

On the first day of school, my students fill out a general information sheet. What they reveal about themselves, their expectations and their fears can be startling.

Some students write me their version of "I'm bad." One student wrote, "I failed English last year. My buds and I got suspended for tying up a substitute teacher and setting her on fire."

They reveal their fears. One high school senior related, "I showed my schedule to some friends in the cafeteria. They said they felt sorry for me because I'd never be able to pass this class."

My physical appearance brought one reaction from a ninth grade boy, "When I first saw you, I thought, 'She must be strict cause she's got her hair up.' "

Another student wrote, "It's good to be in a classroom where the teacher is organized for a change."

One important question on the survey received a variety of responses. It was, "What one thing happened to you this summer that had an impact on your life and you'd like me to know about it."

A senior answered that over the summer she had lost her mother to cancer. Knowing that pertinent information early on helped me relate to her better.

## A Teacher's Reputation

Your reputation precedes you. Principals, colleagues, parents and students all talk about you. The underground network works during lunch and in the hallways. Your former students act like veterans filling in the new recruits. It makes no sense to be a teacher who students don't want as their teacher.

## A Teacher's Appearance

Sales personnel in expensive department stores follow strict dress codes. Managers realize that sales clerks must dress appropriately to make sales. That first day, teachers are selling their authority and competence to students. Within the first six to nine seconds, we're judged. Are your clothes projecting the proper image?

When was the last time you saw your airline pilot board the plane in a cotton jogging outfit and sneakers?

Casual attire (yes, including faded, baggy jeans) are better on weekends than weekdays.

Wearing an outfit that conveys self-respect and personal power improves classroom discipline.

### Proper attire for women:
a suit, a tailored dress, a blazer and slacks, a jacket and skirt or a pant suit

### Proper attire for men:
a dress shirt and trousers, a tie, a blazer and shirt with collar, wrinkle free trousers

The authority on the power of dressing is clothing consultant John T. Molloy. In his classic *The Woman's Dress for Success Book*, he wrote, "The color, pattern and cut of a teacher's clothes affect the attitude, attention span and conduct of high school and junior high school students...

"An outfit can be one teacher's salvation and another's downfall. Women in their 40's and 50's wearing soft, feminine clothes impressed students as authoritative mother figures. But young women in similar clothes had trouble controlling classes."

The correlation between the teacher's attire and strong discipline was apparent at one high school in my area. The teachers wore casual attire — mostly jeans and T-shirts. When the new principal wished to tighten discipline, he established a teacher dress code. At the opening faculty meeting, he explained that jeans were no longer acceptable. He promised to be in the parking lot on the first school day and send teachers home who were improperly dressed. He did send two teachers home that morning. I'm hearing reports from colleagues that not only is discipline much improved, but faculty morale as well.

If department stores can have dress codes, so can schools. Let's dress well and make proper attire a priority. It's another way to create a good first impression.

## Perfectionism

At the beginning of a school year, feeling overwhelmed is typical. Why? Because there's too much to do. Keep in mind that perfectionism is neurotic behavior. The following list of don'ts and do's will help you feel less over-burdened.

# Day One Don'ts

1. **Don't have a museum-perfect classroom.**
2. **Don't have to-die-for bulletin boards.**
   A bare bulletin board is O.K. and is actually beneficial for children who get overly stimulated.
3. **Don't tell all rules.** Be a maverick. Meet students' needs first. The rules can take a week to explain. Give them like vitamins, one-a-day.
4. **Don't call roll.**
   Use assigned seats and a seating chart.
5. **Don't tolerate disrespect and/or misbehavior on day one.** Unless you plan to put up with this inappropriate behavior all year long, correct the student now.

# Day One Do's

1. **Do make your room easy to identify.**
2. **Do have a desk for each child.**
3. **Do dress well all year long.**
4. **Do take attendance quietly.**
5. **Do show courtesy, caring and enthusiasm.**

# Smooth Beginnings

## 1. Hand out boarding passes

At the classroom door, hand students a boarding pass with the seat assignment. Check schedules.

**Your most important job that first day is to stand at the door to welcome kids.**

## 2. Give a brief introduction

Take ten minutes or less to introduce the class to you and to the room. State briefly your expectations for the year. Rather than tell kids, show them.

## 3. Use name tags

Have students wear name tags the first week or two. Computer labels are inexpensive and make great name tags. Collect at the end of the period or day. Know most students' names by the first week.

## 4. Create a time-out desk

Place a desk close to you as a time-out desk for students with behavior problems.

## 5. Set up a pick-up table

This is a long table situated near the door. You have begged, borrowed or stolen it during in-service days. Students enter the room and walk past this table. Before the bell rings, train students to pick up folders, quizzes, handouts, textbooks, etc.

# Pick-Up Table Essentials

### Make-Up Folder

This is a bright red folder that contains all handouts, homework schedules and weekly assignments.

### Make-Up Log

This is a bright blue spiral notebook. One student per week writes the day's date plus two sentences about the assignments. Students who are returning from an absence can read about missed assignments from the Make-Up Log. If they have questions, they see the student who wrote the information.

### In Basket

If a child left a paper on my desk in August, we might not find it again until May. Instead, all papers go into the In Basket on the Pick-Up Table. Baskets are clearly marked by class and/or subject.

## 6. Start work immediately

The bell schedule may be off that first week. After students have arrived, start class quickly. This sends the message, "We work in here."

## 7. Write daily flight plans

The overhead projector, computer screen or chalkboard directs the students with the day's assignments. Use short sentences. When a student asks, "What do we do today?" point and say, "That."

## 8. Start with worthwhile work

Challenges inspire. A classroom that asks nothing of students doesn't impress them.

Starting the school year with a fairly tough test worked for one remedial middle school teacher, Louise Johnson. Students were enrolled in her class because they failed a basic skills test the last semester of seventh grade.

Until students in her one semester course took the pre-test, they resented being there. Mrs. Johnson's pre-test showed the students what they didn't know. When they better understood what needed to be accomplished, their attitude improved.

We make a mistake when we tell students that they can do the assignments because the work is easy. When was the last time you were motivated to do work because it was easy?

Tell students the work that you'll give them is difficult, yet you know they can do it.

## 9. Give directions effectively
### Center attention

Allowing students to talk while you give directions will create behavior problems. If you don't get your needs met for order in the classroom, then you can't teach. The first day, train your students to center their attention. Say:

"When my teacher words are in the air, they need to go directly into each and everyone's mind. When you talk and interrupt that flow, then my words can't get through. I am the boss. Right now, my teacher words are more important than your student words. Listen now."

Another phrase that works to focus attention is: "Get your computers activated." The teacher demonstrates with hands spread up in the air, fingers moving.

### Repeat directions back

Ask students to repeat directions back to you. "I've just entered this classroom. Tell me what I'm to work on." It may take three or four responses to get the assignment repeated correctly, but this technique clears up confusion. Use it consistently and you'll be amazed at how well it works.

## 10. Teach classroom procedures

My aunt, Bernadine English, teaches in a community college. She shared with me some insights into her 25-year career. The first day she emphasizes that students must come to class on time. When class starts, she locks the door. "Otherwise," she explained to me, "I have students who will enter the room all during the two-hour block. I've had students sharpen their pencils while I'm lecturing, get up to leave the room, arrive late and explain that they couldn't find a parking space or that they had a flat tire on the way to class."

"They aren't hateful. They just don't have any common sense or simple courtesy. My students don't see their behavior as being distracting or disrespectful. The first class or two, I train them in my expectations. If they're late, they sit outside in the hallway and take notes. Once they realize my parameters, it's miraculous how they arrive on time."

If college students need training, then surely our students need training, too. Make your first request successful. Give general information the first week. Remind students all year long.

### Tell where to turn in papers
Practice the behavior and check the traffic flow.

### Explain make-up work
Use phone mates. During the first week, ask students to select two other classmates and share telephone numbers. After their absence, students call a phone mate to get the missed assignments. Two numbers are better than one just in case a line is busy or the phone mate was absent as well. When students return to class, they have an idea of the missed work.

### Go over dismissal routines
This is the teacher's task. Students need structures for returning materials and gathering belongings.

### Explain how students can help one another
Get students trained to ask one another for help. Let them know that whispering a question is an acceptable way to assist each other.

## 11. Learn students' names
Since our goal is to know many names by the end of the first week, and all names by the end of the second week, the following small group activities can make this goal achievable.

### Introductions

Have students break into teams of two. Sitting knee to knee, have them interview one another and introduce each other to the class. You may wish to structure this assignment by putting appropriate questions on the board and setting a time limit for the interview.

### The Name Game

For this activity, remove name tags. Have students name each person in their row, table or team. Toward the end of the first week, ask a brave volunteer to name everyone in the class. Then, try it yourself. This is a quick and painless way to learn your students' names.

### "One Positive Thing" Activity

Have students introduce themselves to the class by giving their names and one positive thing that has happened to them in the last two weeks.

### Birth Order Activity

Have students break down into birth order groups. These groups include: the first born siblings, middle child, youngest child and only child. Have each group write a list of their five strong areas and five areas that need improvement. Get one representative to share with the large group. Then go over the birth order information in Chapter four of this book. This activity helps establish cooperation and develop friendships.

With planning and thought, your first week will run smoothly and, in the process, make your classroom marketable and salable to kids.

# Student Information Sheet

Name_____

Name you like to be called_____

Address_____ Telephone_____

Do you work outside of school? ☐ Yes ☐ No

If so, where?_____ Telephone_____

Parents or guardians_____

Place of their employment: _____

Parents/guardians work telephone: _____

1. List brothers/sisters living at home with you?

   <u>Name</u>                    <u>Age</u>_____

   _____

   _____

2. Do you have brothers or sisters living somewhere else? Explain. _____

3. What one thing happened to you this summer that had an impact on your life and you'd like me to know about? Or, what's the best thing that happened in the last two months? _____

4. What would you most like for me, your teacher, to know about you? _____

5. What do you hope to gain from the course? Write one or two major goals. _____

6. List and briefly describe yourself outside of school. Include your interests, sports, hobbies, recreational activities, etc. _____

7. Write the title of your most recently read book or favorite magazine? _____

8. Write a short paragraph of 5-8 sentences on your favorite T.V. program or movie.

   _____

   _____

# Smooth Beginnings

1. Hand out boarding passes.
2. Give a brief introduction.
3. Use name tags.
4. Create a time-out desk.
5. Set up a pick-up table.
6. Start work immediately.
7. Write daily flight plans.
8. Start with worthwhile work.
9. Give effective directions.
10. Demonstrate first week procedures.
11. Learn names and build cooperation.

## Summary

1. Appear organized.
2. Get students in the right room.
3. Have students face you.
4. Get kids working.
5. Take attendance.
6. Impress unobtrusively.
7. Manage with an invisible hand.
8. Remember your reputation.
9. Wear proper attire.

27

# 3

# *Becoming The*
# *Authentic Teacher*

The Authentic Teacher works in harmony with his or her personality, spirit or character. For the authentic teacher, disciplining students is a welcomed challenge.

## Activate Learners

To activate kids, we need to relate well to students and encourage classroom participation. Let's teach less by chance and more by design. The FPAA Fuery Learning Model helps to jump-start learners of any age.

The model is based on the secondary schools' 55-minute period. Make adjustments for your school schedule.

## Fuery Learning Model

**F = Focus**          Suggested time: five minutes

First, get kids focused quickly. Immediately tell students what work they will do and how they will do it. Start with an anecdote, a cartoon on an overhead, a quiz, a puzzle, a surprise, etc. anything that focuses learners.

**P = Participate**    Suggested time: 35 minutes

Have students work on a computer, listen to a presentation, watch a video, listen to a tape, write a paper, etc. In this stage, students participate in activities individually or in teams.

**A = Activate**    Suggested time: five minutes

Too often, teachers skip this stage of the process. Kids need to talk about what they have learned and reflect on their feelings. Allow learners to discuss in pairs or groups.

Stimulate discussion with questions:

What do you think about this assignment?

What are your thoughts and feelings?

What did you learn?

Any questions, comments or concerns?

(I frequently use this last question in my discipline seminars.)

**A = Apply**    Suggested time: ten minutes

Students make an analysis, explain and apply what they've learn. Evaluate with questions such as:

How does this apply to yesterday?

What did you learn or re-learn today?

The last question in the application phase initiates a great review. Each student answers aloud, "What did I learn or re-learn today?

When I give motivational seminars for teachers, many times I'll end with that last important question. Then the microphone is passed around the auditorium and the seminar content is reviewed.

## Break Down Barriers

The moment genuine teachers come up with good ideas that help kids, the negative remarks begin. Why? Because they're threatening the status quo. The more resistance to the idea, the better the idea. Creativity and change aren't the norms in classrooms.

## Barriers To Change

**It's not in the curriculum.**
**You can't teach that.**
**That goes against school policy.**
**It won't work.**
**They will never let you do that.**
**It costs too much.**
**We tried that last year.**

Help the kids in your a classroom by breaking down these barriers.

## Relish Change

Change is uncomfortable and painful. It is easier to keep in the same rut than to blaze a path into uncharted territory. Authentic teachers are courageous pioneers.

Some of the ideas in this book may be new to you, or they may remind you of a teaching technique you've forgotten that worked. Try one new idea a week. Make this year better because you have the self-esteem to experiment. Take risks. Grow.

## Kelsey's Camping Trip

My friend's ninth grade daughter signed up for a school sponsored Outward-Bound canoe trip in the Florida Everglades. After her teachers had talked about the adventure, Kelsey was eager to go. Her mother paid over $800. Then the trouble began.

Before her departure, Kelsey came home every day for two weeks moaning about the hardships.

Frowning at the dinner table one evening, Kelsey groaned, "The campers eat canned meat. They sleep on the ground. The counselors won't allow make-up or boom boxes. And there's no T.V. Only nerds are going on this trip." The litany of complaints continued until, Barbara, Kelsey's mother had enough.

"Well, I've paid the money. You are going, and that's final. I don't want to hear one more word."

It was 5:30 A.M. and the first day of spring break. Barbara and her husband, Brock, loaded a silent, sullen and reluctant camper into the family car and headed for school. After five days, the parents were back at school to meet the bus. Two girls came off the bus first, saw their parents and burst into tears.

When their daughter emerged, Kelsey was sunburned, bruised and bitten by bugs. Her hair was dirty and tangled but she was smiling. She wanted to know when she could go again.

She explained that the group canoed, hiked and camped in remote areas of the Everglades. Every night, they set up camp and shared the cooking chores. On their first day out, two canoes were entangled in a mangrove maze of branches. Instead of wading in the water and working the canoe free, two spoiled and catered-to girls yelled for help. Kelsey and a companion pulled the pampered free. A few kids refused to eat. "That was stupid. No one cared it you ate or not. They just went hungry."

"Once I got to know them, some of the nerds turned out to be really nice," said Kelsey. This young woman returned from the Florida swamp with a new appreciative attitude.

## Make Small Changes

Change helps us teach and reach kids. If we find that our discipline strategies, though successful for the last 10 years, aren't working now, we need to change. The students have changed. We need to keep up.

Sometimes small teacher changes can have a great impact on the ways kids behave.

The following strategies share the teaching and keeps students involved and on-task. Kids who like the work in your room, don't have time to tear down the walls.

## Cooperative Homework

Vary your homework assignments by using a buddy system. Allow students to work in two-person teams. Encourage students to meet after class and work on projects.

Another cooperative homework assignment is to require students to interview family or community members, write about their discoveries and share this information with the class.

## Group Work

At times, students learn more easily from each other than they do from the teacher. Encourage them to brainstorm to generate new ideas. Teach students the use of eye contact, how their body language conveys interest, and the power of reflective listening to promote understanding within a group.

Tell students to do their fair share because they are no longer working for the teacher but for themselves and the good of the team. Let them know in advance they'll get rewarded, recognized and praised.

Kids need to learn to work smarter rather than harder. Set a time limit that creates urgency. Monitor the groups by floating from group to group to keep them on task.

# Manage Class Discussions

Class discussions are essential for getting students excited, interacting and thinking. Some guidelines include:

## 1. Ask open-ended questions

Start discussions with a question for the entire class and wait for a response. Students need time. Eventually they will answer.

"What did you think about the disaster in today's newspaper? Did it make you more aware of something?"

"What did you think about the homework assignment? Did anyone learn anything new? Did you like it?"

## 2. Ask permission

Use phrases like: "Perhaps, Mary, you might like to answer this question?"

"I was wondering, George, if you'd consider this question?"

Tell students to raise their hand as a fist if they don't want to be called on.

## 3. Don't stop a discussion

If students' responses indicate you need to teach certain materials again, include it in your lesson plans a short time later.

## 4. Eliminate evaluation of responses

Use reflective listening by rephrasing what students say. Respond with, "I hear you saying.....is that true?"

"I'm glad you raised that point."

## 5. Listen to feelings and facts

Let students know you may not agree with their opinions but you're willing to listen to their feelings.

Respond with feedback that encourages honesty.

"The homework bored you?"

"Could you let me know why?"

"You're glad you're finished with that paper."

"You feel strongly about this issue."

By activating learners, accepting minor behavior imperfections, breaking down the barriers to trying new ideas and relishing change, the authentic teacher relates positively in a caring, loving way toward students.

# Summary
**The Authentic Teacher**
1. Activates learners.
2. Accepts minor behavior imperfections.
3. Breaks down barriers.
4. Relishes change.

**The FPAA Learning Model:**
F = Focus
P= Participate
A= Activate
A= Apply

**Manage Class Discussions**
1. Ask open-ended questions.
2. Eliminate evaluation of responses.
3. Listen to feelings and facts.

36

# 4

# *Projecting The*
# *Prizefighter Image*

The winning prizefighter wears a red satin jacket to get beat-up. He brags about his ability to turn opponents into hamburger and accepts compliments automatically.

Behind closed dressing room doors, the stage for battle is set. The prizefighter emerges to face fears, foes and fans with cocky confidence. If we can project some of the bravado of a winning prizefighter, we'll do better in the discipline arena.

## A Reputation for Boldness

"Whatever you can do, or dream you can ... begin it. Boldness has genius, power and magic in it."

Goethe

A general level of cowardice prevails in schools and in teaching. Acquiring a reputation for boldness is easy. Incredibly enough our students will generally accept an order expressed with self-confidence.

In the book *Do It!* by John-Roger and Peter McWilliams, a quote by Margo Kaufman grabbed my attention.

"I once complained to my father that I didn't seem to be able to do things the same way other people did. Dad's advice? 'Margo, don't be a sheep. People hate sheep. They eat sheep.' "

Teachers with strong self-esteem aren't like other teachers. Kids consume weak teachers for lunch.

Weak teachers are fragile and insecure. They appear tough outwardly, but they're threatened by students. They wonder about the value of their lessons. They're fearful of slipping, of letting down their guard and showing students a glimpse of the real person hiding behind the mask of superiority.

Strong teachers take risks and experiment. They are bold and act with conviction. Strong teachers know what their needs are and don't expect students to fill them. They are confident of their decisions.

## Act Directly

Soon after the Unity Church of Naples, Florida, was built down an unpaved and unnamed road, the church members realized they needed to give their street a name. Instead of meeting with the county commissioners to ask permission to install a sign, the church officials hired a sign maker. They erected an expensive-looking sign.

When the map makers came out from the county offices, they found the street sign and said, "Oh, this must be Unity Way." The church officials knew about the rewards of acting directly. Powerful leaders know it's always better to beg forgiveness than to ask permission.

Michael Korda in his book *Success!* wrote about an executive who also never asked permission. He came to work for a large firm. Strict rules governed who signed check vouchers and contract authorizations. Only vice-presidents were allowed this privilege.

The new employee observed that everyone in his department followed this protocol, but he decided to ignore it. He signed everything with the final touch of a rubber stamp that read, "authorized". No one objected to his assumptions. Soon fellow executives were bringing him papers to sign, and he was discussed as a young man to be watched and groomed for higher management.

## Get Rid of "Just"

How many times at a convention have I asked the person sitting next to me, "What do you do?", only to receive the lowered voice, the down-cast eyes, "Oh, I'm just a teacher." I hear that so often that I now respond with "Get rid of the 'just.' "

Pride and conviction make a huge difference to the response, "I'm a teacher."

Recognize and take responsibility for the way words affect our personal power. Our words filter through our subconscious and become part of our character. If we're serious about projecting power, we need to take charge of our mouths.

Speak positively. It takes discipline and effort, but it's simple. Monitoring what we say and think requires us to be different from the herd. Excellence always does.

# Daily Affirmations

After our alarm clock rings, early morning thoughts help or hinder our confidence. Daily affirmations, positive thoughts we repeat to ourselves, allow us to plant messages in our subconscious. These messages help us teach better.

## Words To Teach By

**I am a good teacher. I am enough.**
**I am capable, caring and professional.**
**I like what I do, and I do it well.**
**During tough times, I let go and let God.**
**I create my own reality.**
**I am responsible for my happiness.**
**Life is good, and this moment is the best.**
**Each day, I begin again. Today is a good day.**
**I project confidence. I'm taking charge.**
**I'm doing what needs to be done.**

Affirmations need to be stated in the positive. "I won't argue with my students" is a poor affirmation because your subconscious mind doesn't hear "not". When you say the affirmation aloud, you involve more of your senses.

Some of my favorite affirmations are posted on my desk and bathroom mirror. I read them everyday. My opinion of me is much more important than anyone else's. When we decide our self-image, we also determine our worth and how much happiness and success we can expect.

Our self-image is our thermostat. We continue to perform within the self-prescribed range.

## Your Self-Esteem

In the movie *Sister Act*, the Mother Superior is an older, set-in-her-ways, bitter nun. She is not happy with the changes that Sister Mary Clarence (Whoopie Goldberg) is making. Sister Mary is a call girl getting police protection by posing as a nun and choir director.

Sister Mary has been informed that she'll be leaving the convent soon. A heated discussion begins in the convent's office.

"I'm leaving," says the Mother Superior.

"That makes two of us," answers Sister Mary Clarence. (Whoopie Goldberg).

"I've asked to be relocated. I must go where I can be of some use. I have been here for years. I've become somewhat obsolete."

"You don't have to continue being obsolete. You are a formidable woman. You could keep this going."

"I am a relic," answers Sister Mary. "And I've misplaced my tambourine."

### The Relic

The older nun saw herself as a relic — useless and worn-out. Still a formidable woman, her thermostat was stuck. She was ready to give up. Until the view of herself changed, there would be no improvements.

The world is a reflection of ourselves. When we hate ourselves, we also hate everyone else.

When we love being who we are, the rest of the world is wonderful. People who see themselves as relics are stuck in old patterns.

## Make a Grand Entrance

Your first five minutes at school sets the tone for the day. From the moment your foot hits the pavement in the teacher's parking lot, you're making a statement.

Move decisively. Look as if you are on your way to something important. Whether heading for the office or the bathroom, successful teachers walk at a fast, purposeful pace.

Posture counts. Your entire body portrays energy. Stand tall with shoulders back and a bearing that says to students, "I mean business here." Powerful posture means pulling in your stomach, standing erect, moving briskly, holding your head up, squaring your shoulders and evenly dividing your weight between both feet.

If you insist on carrying papers home, put them in a briefcase or a carrying case that zips neatly. Don't carry an open satchel with papers falling out. How you carry your school materials should look as professional as your apparel.

## Smile, Greet Everyone

Say hello to everyone. Greet the person in the office by name. Smile at everyone. It gives your face something to do. Don't be accused of having your smile surgically removed. Get to school in enough time to use the bathroom, look over the days work and prepare the room. When the opening bell rings, stand at your door. Shake hands. Touch students with your smile and words.

## Jacket with "The Attitude"

It was Christmas time and my teenage son, Scott, took a date to the mall for some last minute shopping. Scott has broad shoulders, stands 6'2", lives in a black leather jacket and drives a motorcycle. He and his girlfriend headed for the food court, and it was crowded.

At tables along one wall sat three young men, each at his own table. With their backs to Scott, they were sprawled out, laughing and shouting back and forth to one another. Food wrappers, empty paper cups and plates covered the table nearest my son.

Without a word, Scott took his arm and raked all the paper wrappings to the floor. The three young men looked dismayed, stood up as if to say something, and then walked away.

After they were out of sight, Scott quickly picked up the mess he'd created. I asked him how he had the nerve to do something like that. He answered, "I had on my Harley Davidson jacket. It's my jacket with the attitude."

Our self-esteem is the jacket with the attitude.

Whether the jacket is red satin or black leather, our attitude is one more power tool for the prizefighter.

## Stand Throughout the Room

Stand with your weight balanced on both feet. Keep your hands out of your pockets. Uncross your arms and legs. Make your arm gestures sure and certain.

Look students in the eyes, and ask them to do the same. Leave your wimp voice at home. Vary your voice tone. Project your voice so that you are easily heard throughout the room.

Move quickly from the front to the back of the room. Watch the attention level increase. If you have a podium, stand in front of it. Stand in front of your desk. Wear a jacket to project weight and authority.

## Automatic Pilot

All of us know teachers who work on automatic pilot. They've taught the same way for so long that it no longer requires their conscious brains. They retire at age 26 but don't leave the building until they're 65. Everyone suffers. We need to get out of the comfortable rut and head for the open road.

Too many of us live on automatic pilot. We get up, fix breakfast, drive to work, teach, return home, fix dinner, watch television, sleep — all in a self-induced coma. We don't share feelings and we don't look at one another. We don't even realize we aren't living consciously.

Susan is a friend whose husband is addicted to daily news reports. One morning as they were blindly going through the rituals, television blaring and newspapers on the breakfast table, Susan realized they were not seeing one another. The next day she tried an experiment. She made coffee and set the table wearing just a pointed paper birthday hat. Nothing else.

Her husband didn't notice. She asked him about the weather. She asked if he wanted hot or cold cereal. For five minutes they talked, while he sat reading the paper. It wasn't until she pulled a chair up beside him, that he finally looked at her.

## Living Consciously

You choose whether to live in automatic pilot or fully conscious. Your survival depends on getting out of automatic pilot, trying something new and feeling fully alive.

If you're pouring a cup of coffee, scrambling an egg, setting an alarm clock or kissing a loved one — all these activities can be carried out with a clear focus and the care they deserve. Your flow of attention is your life. Use it with awareness. Your flow of attention is your greatest treasure.

I was giving a closing keynote address to about 600 female cafeteria workers. I asked the listeners what pleasurable thing they anticipated at the end of the convention. I passed the microphone around so that their statements could be heard.

One woman said that she planned to go to a flea market and another lady had arranged for her husband to take her to a romantic restaurant for dinner. A third lady, who looked a little on the grand motherly side, said clearly and with conviction into the microphone, "I plan to do Alfonso."

Now, I don't know Alfonso, but from the reaction in the room, I'd say that "doing Alfonso" ranks right up there with one of life's greatest pleasures.

Lily Tomlin, the comedian, says there will be sex after death, we just won't be able to feel it. Feeling things is one of our natural-given pleasures. Let's not miss out.

One way to cut pleasure from life is to deny compliments. Ever tell a friend, "My you look super in that peach jacket," only to have her respond, "Why this old thing? I just pulled it from the goodwill bag this morning. Been meaning to give it away for years."

Prizefighters put pleasure in their lives and take compliments as their due. If we project the confidence and bravado of a prizefighter, we'll win more battles.

## Summary

**Prizefighter Teachers**

1. **Create a bold reputation.**
2. **Act directly and say positive things.**
3. **Believe in daily affirmations.**
4. **Enhance self-esteem.**
5. **Make a grand entrance. Greet everyone.**
6. **Wear a jacket with an attitude.**
7. **Stand throughout the room.**
8. **Add pleasure.**

# 5

## *Birth Order:*
## *You, Me And The Kids*

$O$ur original classroom is our family of origin. Birth order — first born, middle child, youngest or only child — creates our personalities. We can learn valuable lessons from understanding our students' and our own family roles.

## Why Study Birth Order?

We can use birth order information to increase self-awareness and to help us connect. A wise counselor at my high school in Fort Myers, Florida, was responsible for enrolling new students. I watched Mr. Bromley work.

When a teenager appeared in his office — shy, insecure and fearful — Mr. Bromley discovered immediately if he/she was first born, middle, youngest or an only child.

Within moments tension and insecurity melted as both laughed over a "perfect" older brother or a "center of attention" baby sister.

By relating to birth order, this counselor created an immediate comfort zone. He showed students he cared and sent them into unfamiliar territory with renewed courage and confidence.

## Resolve Problems

One year I taught a fourth-hour, "low ability" 12th grade English class. The reading levels varied from non-readers to about sixth grade level. Most of my students had failed English courses in the past. Some were mainstreamed from special education classes. One of my brightest students could barely write a sentence, yet he captivated the class with his amazing insights.

I dreaded my reluctant learners. I had students who drank beer before class. Several used and sold drugs. I began the year with 25 students, 23 were boys.

The boys' testosterone level was as high as salmon rushing up stream. Another teacher, who had taught most of these kids in previous years, looked at my roll during the first day of classes and asked, "What did you do to deserve this?" I checked the absentee sheet daily with hopes that two or three would be suspended.

My school was severely overcrowded and many teachers floated like transient campers. It didn't help that I used another teacher's classroom for my fourth-hour group. I remember racing to class to beat my students because if I arrived late, they usually beat on each other.

As I got to know them better, I discovered that all but three were the youngest in their families. They were used to getting their way. They knew how to manipulate adults.

### "Why did you give me a hard time?"

Toward the end of the year, I had established a rapport with most of the students. I asked them why, in the beginning of the year, they had given me such a hard time. I was amazed at their reactions.

With sly smiles on their faces, they explained that when I was upset, I was so much fun to watch. I was their entertainment. They loved the show. If I had known in the beginning that they were mostly last born, I would have used a different approach.

## Basics

Every seven years, the family begins a new constellation. This means if you have two older sisters and the closest in age to you is ten years apart, you're considered a first born. You may possess some characteristics of the youngest, but overall your birth order is first.

The birth order descriptions may not fit you or your students perfectly, but they will give insights you'll find beneficial for handling your special clients.

## Oldest Child/Only Child

According to the book, *Birth Order and You*, more than half the presidents of the United States were oldest children.

One elementary teacher reports that she has her students form into groups during the first weeks of school. Oldest siblings dictate orders and tell other students what to do.

Generally, oldest children are highly motivated and like structure and order. They receive the undiluted power of their parents' love plus their parents' fears. With high parental expectations, they receive harsher punishment and are pushed to excel.

In high school, my older brother ran track. If he wasn't standing in the parking lot when my dad arrived to take him home, he ran an additional six miles to our house. He received the full force of my father's impatience. By the time my youngest brother came along, Dad was much more relaxed.

## Here Comes Competition

The shock of a new baby is best described in Adele Faber and Elaine Mazlish's book, *Siblings Without Rivalry*. Imagine, the authors explain, that your husband announces he's bringing home a new, younger wife. He gives her his full attention and time. She gets some of your clothes. He asks you to watch over her while he's at work.

Because they feel replaced, many oldest children become hostile or revert back to baby-like behavior. To win back lost attention, they try harder to be perfect.

## The Enforcer

Because the oldest sometimes becomes a deputy parent, he/she may earn the nickname, the Enforcer. By the age of ten, my oldest brother, Jimmy, baby-sat for me and my two other brothers. He was a power monger. There was the Christmas morning he wouldn't let us open presents until our beds were made. Once when he was babysitting he waved his Boy Scout hatchet above our unruly skulls.

Parents reward the enforcer and appreciate the cooperation. My oldest brother still loves to tell me what to do and would gladly run my life for me.

## Our Personal Relationships

My cousin, Chuck, was a first born. After his second divorce, he figured out why his two wives had left. He rescued broken birds — women whose lives needed lots of devotion, direction and support. Once they got back on their feet, they no longer needed a father figure. And Chuck was left without a wife.

He is now in a healthier relationship with a woman who is independent, successful and secure. Last spring, she flew them to Paris for his birthday. He later confessed he had a difficult time being the one cared for. He is getting used to it now, and his relationship is thriving. The research indicates that first borns take responsibility for other people's lives. That was certainly true in Chuck's case.

## Self-Evaluation: Adult Oldest

Are you a perfectionist?
Can you admit when you are wrong?
Can you accept constructive criticism?
Are you accused of being bossy?

## Coping Strategies

Set the example by admitting mistakes.
Apologize when you're wrong.
Encourage playfulness and risk-taking.
Let students know perfection isn't required.

# Middle Child

Middle children are like Avis — always number two. They try harder. The second child, especially of the same sex, will compete for mom and dad's attention. Middle children are forced to compete with a younger, cuter sibling. The closer in age to the oldest, the stronger the competitive instincts.

## Same Sex Children

With same sex children, the middle child receives the least attention and affirmation from parents. As a result, the second born may become hostile and argumentative just to be noticed.

My neighbors have three girls ages five, seven and ten. The middle child, Christina, craves attention and openly competes with Heather, her talented, older sister. Christina is stubborn and a fighter. The girls argue continually.

I see this competitive spirit in my own family. My two older brothers, Jim and Bill are only two years apart yet they're still competing to see who is the strongest and the toughest. Today, as two middle age men, they challenge each other on ski slopes, tennis courts and football fields. The competition hasn't ended.

## Odd Man Out

If the middle child feels left out, he/she may be justified by knowing that middle children have fewer pictures in the photo albums or home videos.

The most monogamous of all birth orders, middle children are last to seek the counsel of helping professions. They are the last to seek a divorce. They didn't fit into their own family, so they are reluctant to break up the family they created.

## Family Outside the Family

According to Dr. Kevin Leman in *The Birth Order Book*, middle children form a family outside the family. They develop many friendships and become good team players.

Because they make friends quickly at school and in their neighborhoods, they fit best with their peers. Some become rebels and free spirits and reject the family's do's and don'ts. They are sensitive to being left out. Early in life, they learned to get their way through compromise and negotiation. Middle siblings become great negotiators and mediators. They're adept at dealing with a variety of people.

## Middle Children As Adults

The training they received as children helps in relationships. Accepting of others, they may be happier because of lower expectations. As a drawback, they avoid conflict. Resentments accumulate to the point where it becomes too late to save the marriage or relationship.

As a middle sibling, I struggled to maintain my 22 year marriage. I refused counseling until a year of pain made my situation unbearable. I made the mistake of thinking I could fix my marriage. It is not wise to think we can solve all our problems without help.

# Self Evaluation: Middle Children

Are you still competing with an older sibling?
Do you hesitate to share your opinion?
Do you need affirmation and praise?
Are you avoiding conflicts?

# Teacher Coping Strategies

Encourage students to share honest thoughts.

Realize that in their efforts to please us, they may leave out important feelings.

Avoid comparing him/her to a smarter, better behaved brother or sister.

# The Beautiful Baby

Youngest children are special members of the family. They may be treated like the family pet or mascot, and they often get lots of attention. Everyone feels responsible for taking care of the youngest. Parents describe the youngest as the most fun to be with and the easiest to raise.

Youngest kids are optimists and hedonists. They expect good things to happen to them. By looking helpless, they can get others to rush to their aid. Because they are the smallest, they learn early to manipulate, pout or use charm to get their way.

# Rules Have Less Meaning

Youngest children receive less discipline and physical punishment than other siblings. Older brothers or sisters may resent that laxness and feel that the youngest gets away with everything.

Rules have less meaning for the youngest child. Inclined to break social rules, they think rules are meant for others. In their personal life, last borns are likely to procrastinate and be late for appointments.

# Creating Ambivalence

My screaming-for-attention, fourth-hour class of last borns could be charming and endearing one moment and rebellious and hard to deal with the next. Their ambivalent nature made me feel out of control. Last borns tend to be followers more than leaders. In looking for praise and encouragement, he/she can be charming, outgoing and affectionate, as well as critical, temperamental, spoiled and impatient.

# Self-Evaluation: Adult Youngest

Do others do too much for you?

Do you accept full responsibility for yourself?

Are you aware of your gifts to be funny, charming and persuasive?

# Teacher Coping Strategies

Give positive praise and admiration.

The student's goal is approval from peers.

Let them know they have to behave or they'll be removed from the group.

Make demands. Make them responsible.

# Only Children

"Hell is other people."

Jean-Paul Sartre, philosopher

Psychologist G. Stanley Hall made the statement, "Being an only child is a disease in itself."

Actually the recent research shows only children are as well adjusted as those with siblings. Many of their personality traits are similar to the first born.

The only child is considered special and precious by generally older parents. He/she has less resentment of authority than a youngest child, and expects and accepts help from others. Usually an only child has high self-esteem. He/she never competes, and therefore doesn't fight for the attention of a friend. He/she simply moves on to someone else.

## Competing with Mom for Dad

The only child sometimes competes with the same sex parent for the attention of the other parent.

Growing up, my family was close to another family with an only son about the age of my younger brother. I always found it odd that the son, Sammy, sat in the front seat with his mother, while the father rode like a child in the back seat. Sammy competed with his father for the mother's attention.

Many only children wish there were a brother or sister to share the parental focus. One friend of mine, an only child now in her 40's, said she had this fantasy when growing up that both her parents would be killed in an auto accident. She was adopted by a television type, picture perfect family. This longing for siblings is typical of only children.

## Super-Perfectionist

Parents of only children are generally older, well educated and successful. They are more set in their ways. They expect a child to fit neatly into their highly structured lifestyle.

This creates a child who is a super-perfectionist; one who gets extremely intolerant and impatient. Only children often wish, when seeing things not done to their liking, that they could go in, take over and do things the right way.

They also become super-conscientious. They do what they say they will do. They appear articulate and mature, yet under the facade, they feel they aren't quite good enough.

## Self Evaluation: Only Children

Are you overly critical? Do you allow students to make mistakes?

In groups, do you wish to move in, take over and do the work yourself?

Do you set unrealistic expectations?

## Coping Strategies

Encourage students to view small disagreements as a part of life.

Encourage spontaneity, team work, flexibility and peer interaction.

# Twins

Much of the development of twins depends on how parents feel about and deal with having twins. In families where the parents emphasize that one child was born before the other, even just a few minutes, the oldest may take the role of older brother or sibling.

Friends of mine, now in their mid-20's were born just six minutes apart. George is the "older" responsible brother, and Richard is the "in need of looking after" younger sibling.

George is an attractive, happily married teacher. His parents call him and ask him to run errands on Saturdays. His wife wonders why his twin, Richard can't help his parents.

"No one expected too much of Richard," says George. "I was repeatedly reminded that I was born first and needed to be the one in charge. Of course, both my parents were first borns."

"If there are other children in the family, twins will have most of the characteristics of the birth position they share," explains Dr. Ronald Richardson in the book, *Birth Order And You*.

Dr. Richardson continues, "Since twins twice as often hear the word, 'no' from their parents, they can easily ignore commands. Each pretends the message is for the other twin. They may not feel the need to try hard in school or excel. Being part of a twin is special enough."

They may also rely on one another so much that they don't make the effort to get along with others. Girl twins develop the closest relationship with each other. This need for closeness may be a threat to marriages that involve a twin.

Twin siblings are expected to share everything. Fairness becomes a big issue for adult twins. They become overly sensitive to any slight or the appearance of being given less time or attention than someone else. Because as children they didn't share willingly, possessions and ownership become overly important.

If you're a twin, and there are no other children in the family, you'll act like two siblings without the age conflict. In families where parents emphasize that one was born before the other, the older may take the role of the oldest. He/she will treat the younger twin like a younger sibling. If twins have other siblings, they'll have the characteristics of the birth position they share.

Now that you know the birth order basics, you may wish to share this information with your classes. As much as it helps you understand yourself, it will help your students understand themselves.

# Summary

1. Oldest child
   highly motivated,
   likes structure and order,
   pushes to excel,
   perfectionist, deputy parent,
   takes on responsibility for others.

2. Middle child
   rebel, free spirit,
   forms family outside family,
   great negotiator, many friends,
   team player, avoids conflicts
   seeks affirmation and praise.

3. Youngest child
   family pet, mascot,
   optimist, hedonist, outgoing,
   gets less discipline, procrastinates,
   breaks social rules, craves respect,
   charming yet rebellious.

4. Only child
   super-perfectionist, dependable,
   has imaginary friends,
   likes structure.

61

# 6

## _Games Kids Play_

Students play a variety of games with their teachers. Most of the games are extremely subtle.

A game is a contest with rules. The players agree to the rules, then one side tries to win. Caught unaware, teachers reward students for inappropriate behavior. By recognizing when a game is being played, we can reduce the reward and turn these situations into positive contests with positive results.

### Avoidance Games

"I need to go to the....clinic, bathroom, hall, my last class, cafeteria, office, my car, telephone, locker, etc."

"I don't have my pencil, paper, textbook, book-bag..."

### Explanation

This game gives the student a chance to avoid failure. He/she reasons, "I couldn't do the work, teacher, I was at my locker, in the clinic, etc. If I don't have a pencil or text, I'll give up. I won't try, then failure was not my fault. The student is discouraged and feels inadequate and reasons it's better not to try than to be embarrassed.

# Teacher Strategies

## 1. Say "No"

The easy answer for a request to leave the room is "No." You can say it sweetly. It is a complete sentence. It needs no explanation. Keep calm.

## 2. Emergency Bathroom Pass

Keep a bathroom pass on the desk. Have very stringent rules regarding its use. Let's face life. At home, a 12-year-old doesn't have to ask permission to go to the bathroom. Bathroom use is a necessity; asking an adult to use the toilet can be demeaning.

My students have permission to use the bathroom pass when needed. A student using the pass simply waves or shows it to me as he/she heads out the door. I don't make a big deal about it and they don't either. The pass is not overused because I've explained the guidelines early in the year.

## 3. Class Bathroom Trip

When I team-taught eighth grade middle school, another teacher and I had a two hour block of time each day. At the end of the first hour, the class went to the bathroom and drinking fountain as a group.

Elementary classes do this all the time. It's less distracting than kids leaving the room one at a time, and prevents students from stretching a five-minute trip into a 25-minute excursion.

## 4. Supply Missing Items

Keep extra pens, pencils, paper and a few textbooks handy for lending. Keep tissues and bandages inside the desk to decrease trips to the clinic. Quietly ask another student for the missing items. Thank the student. This solution gets kids working. Comedian, Woody Allen, said, "Most of life is just showing up." If I can get kids to show up, even if I occasionally have to provide a few tools, I'll be happy and so will they.

## 5. Keep Class Notebooks

Students keep a notebook in the classroom that contains a pen, pencil and paper. Notebooks are locked in file drawers. Before class, I spread these notebooks out on a table near the door. Students pick up their notebooks as they enter the classroom. When the bell rings, they have most of what they need.

# Power Games

"You're so mean."
"I hate this class!"
"This class sucks."
"This is a retarded class. When can I get out?"
"You can't make me."
"You can't do nothing to me."
"All we get are stupid assignments in here."

# Explanation

These games are meant to defeat us. They cover up unspoken messages that hide students' real feelings. If a student could express his emotions appropriately, he'd say, "This threatens me. I am afraid I'll fail. I'm afraid to try. I'm discouraged and fearful. The only way I count is if I stand up to the teacher."

The student is hostile, defiant and resistant and won't cooperate when corrected. Other expressions include disobedience, pouting or lying.

## Teacher Strategies

We cannot deny children's feelings. We don't have to agree, but we can accept their right to feel, and we can clarify their remarks so we understand one another better. By mirroring the feelings of the students, we can get their hidden feelings out in the open.

## The Mirroring Technique

This is a communication skill used by therapists. It's simple and it works.

In your ninth grade English class a student announces, "I hate this class." Stand close to the student. Paraphrase his remark and ask for a confirmation. "You really detest the work in this class. Am I understanding you correctly?"

"Yes. Especially that stupid essay we had to write last night. I only got half a page."

"So, you're telling me that the essay assignment was so stupid you could only think of half a page to write. Am I hearing you ?"

"Yeah, here it is. And it stinks."

"Let me take a look at it. You know a lot of times I think my own writing stinks, too."

At this point, you've allowed some real feelings to be heard. Be sure to use a nonjudgmental and noncritical tone of voice. When the students' feelings have been made clear, when they feel you've listened, you reduce the hostility.

However, if you're angry, you won't be able to do this, because an angry teacher makes a poor active listener.

**"Yes, But...I Don't Have Time For This."**

This technique does take a few minutes of your time. But when we deny anger, we spend additional moments dealing with a student's frustrations, usually at the cost of losing valuable teaching time.

You may need to say, "Hold that thought, and we'll talk about it soon." Mean what you say by arranging a few minutes at the end of the period or end of the day to be with that student. If we take the time to listen, kids will know their feelings are understood.

Mirroring works in any relationship. It is an unexpected luxury to have another person's full attention.

A student who is mirrored has more energy because he/she feels understood. Practice the technique with a husband, wife or close friend. The results may surprise you.

# Denial Doesn't Work

Denying feelings doesn't work. Do you recall a time growing up when you expressed a negative feeling such as, "I hate my little brother." Your parent responded with, "Oh, you don't really mean that." We quickly learned to censor our remarks.

We were trained to distrust our instincts. When we deny what we feel, we distort our view of reality. Mirroring works because it says to a child, "It's O.K. to feel. I hear what you are saying, I don't have to agree with you, but I do accept you."

## Apathy Games – Looking Busy

Kids realize early that if they sit behind broad-shouldered Buck or Betty they can get away with anything. If they appear to be working, stay quiet and unnoticed they won't have to do a thing. It's a great avoidance ploy that wastes valuable time.

## Explanation

Resistance can be subtle and covert. With a dominant teacher, a student may feel it's too risky to rebel openly. He may gaze out the window, daydream, skip class or have frequent illnesses. It helps if there is a cooperative parent who writes excused notes from home.

## Fill-In-The-Blanks

I was giving a group of middle school students some information as they jotted notes. I asked them to stop taking notes, look over what they had written and give me their opinion.

One student responded with, "Oh, don't ask us to think about that. Just tell us what you want us to write down." By listening, remaining silent and being told what to do, they avoided thinking.

# Teacher Strategies

## 1. Walk "the beat"

Walk down rows and around groups to make sure every student is on task. Ask to see completed work.

## 2. Sit in the back

Watch and see what students are really doing.

## 3. Know your client

Connect on a personal level with kids. At the beginning of the year, students fill out interest/family information surveys. Beside a student's name in my gradebook, I write notations such as, "volleyball" or "5 sisters". These are facts learned from the survey.

Before class, I ask questions about their lives and relate on a personal level. Students are pleasantly surprised what I know about them. Sometimes they respond with, "How did you know that?" I give them my best Mona Lisa smile and say, "Oh, I have my ways." It pays to be a little mysterious.

# Attention Games

Attention-seeking behaviors include tattling (with younger kids), bizarre dress, unusual hair style, clowning, noisiness, restlessness, showing off for peers, being late for class (so that a grand entrance is possible), etc.

# Explanation

Elementary students want attention from the teacher. Teenagers are more likely to seek recognition from their peers. The better students feel about themselves, the less likely they will be to elevate themselves with a performance.

# Teacher Strategies

## 1. Terminating tattling

Let your class know that each person will get one tattle a day. An elementary teacher explains, "You only get one tattle a day, so you 'd better be careful how you use it. My ears can only take one tattle, after that I'll tell you to take your seat and give your attention to your work."

## 2. Handling bizarre dress/hair style

If the office allows the outfit or hair style you may wish to make a comment such as, "That's an unusual hair style. How did you do it?" Or, "That's a wild outfit. Where did you get it?"

## 3. Be encouraging

Make your screaming-for-attention student the center of attention. Any helping role with visibility works — passing back papers, taking something to the office or doing an errand. Connecting with students on a personal basis-asking about his/her family or sports gives that needed attention.

# Champions

In March of 1994 in Miami, Florida, Pete Sampras became the first back-to-back winner of the Lipton Tennis Championships. Earlier, on that fateful Sunday, Sampras wasn't looking well. He was ill with a stomach virus and was scheduled for his final match with Andre Agassi at one p.m.

When Sampras didn't report for the match within the 15 minutes allowed by Tennis Tour rules, he could have been defaulted. Agassi, hearing of his rival's illness, stopped by the locker room to tell Sampras to take all the time he needed to feel better.

It was a close, emotional match and Sampras won. At the awards ceremony Agassi gave a closing speech.

"You don't deserve to win the tournament unless you can beat the best players. If I couldn't go out there healthy and beat Pete, I don't deserve to win the tournament with him sick. It's not about winning the tournament. It is about taking pride in what you do..."

Andre Agassi

I see the games kids play as a challenge rather than an assault. I win by facing the problems with the courage of a warrior.

We may not always be able to win at the games kids play, but we can take pride in our teaching, succeed with the best strategies and rally with the courage of champions.

# Summary

1. **Avoidance Games**
   Say, "No."
   Have a bathroom pass.
   Supply missing items.
   Keep class notebooks.

2. **Power Games**
   Use the mirroring technique.
   Make the necessary time.

3. **Apathy Games**
   Walk your beat.
   Observe from back of room.
   Know your client.
   Have class discussions.

4. **Attention Games**
   Terminate tattling.
   Handle bizarre appearances.
   Be encouraging.

# 7

# *Discipline Remedies For Reluctant Learners*

We discussed earlier the importance of projecting a powerful, in-charge teacher image. Now we'll portray prizefighter behavior.

## Fix Brush Fires

### 1. Get eye contact

To get students focused on you, say any one of the following statements. Wait in silence while students comply:

"I can't continue until I get your eyes."

"Front and center with your eyes."

"Eyes on me."

"Let's focus our attention here."

"I'll wait until I see your eyes."

Or we can lead with this statement:

"I need for you to look me in the eyes because I teach each and everyone of you. I am your individual teacher. I teach you as a group but also as a unique and special individual."

"I realize that in some cultures, respect for the teacher is shown by not giving eye contact. But in this classroom, giving eye contact is respectful to me."

## 2. Listen with eye contact

I was in a busy restaurant with a handsome, single attorney, Jerry. A female, single friend, Sarah, stopped by our table to chat. We both stood briefly and talked with her. After Sarah left, I told Jerry that she was interested in dating some new men. Did he have any friends who were available? He explained that although he found her quite attractive, he wouldn't be introducing her to any of his colleagues.

Curious, I asked why. At first, he was reluctant but then he explained, "The entire time she spoke with me her eyes flickered. She has wandering eyes. She was looking for something better."

This wonderful man wouldn't be introducing my friend to eligible bachelors because he felt insulted by her flickering eyes. Subconsciously she sabotaged a relationship that may have been helpful.

When we fail to make eye contact with our students, when we talk with them and allow our eyes to wander, we're saying, "You aren't important to me."

Nothing is better for a student's ego than the teacher's undivided attention. It's difficult to give full eye contact when you have a room full of kids also requiring attention, yet we can sabotage our efforts with students by denying them a few moments from our eyes. Active listening requires eye contact.

## 3. Scan

Scan when you work with one group of kids or an individual. About every two to three minutes, look up to check on the group. Scanning keeps you informed of what's happening.

## 4. Clint Eastwood Stare

After scanning, comes "the stare." We've all used "the stare" to get kids back on track. It is effective.

## 5. Get close

Think for a moment about the way we discipline a three-year-old. We take the child onto our lap, put our arms about him or her and speak softly. We look the child in the eyes. We let the child see the pain or anger on our face. The child is being comforted and scolded at the same time. We tell the child how to behave in the future. Whether they are first graders or seniors, we can create similar corrective measures with our students.

Distance is a barrier. Distance will defeat even the best discipline strategy. Kids pretend not to hear you. It's essential to be physically close.

If you are pulling a student aside for a brief conference, both of you should sit. We have the most resistance while standing. That's why taking kids out into the hallway doesn't work. You're both standing. Better to pull up a chair and sit. Give eye contact.

## 6. Use a strong voice

Our voice tone conveys confidence. Leave the wimp, weak voice at home. We need a voice that conveys through our tone, "I know you'll cooperate with me," and "I know you'll do what's right."

Project your voice. Be sure back row Bart can hear. Voice projection and volume mean power. The teacher who can't be heard is weak and ineffective.

# 7. Use the 47-second prompt

Bill Bailey is a fourth grader in your class. You have given the assignment and are walking around the room, answering questions. Bill is too busy to work. His book isn't open, his paper is on the floor and he's turned around in his seat jabbing his fist into the boy behind him. When your Clint Eastwood stare goes unnoticed, you need to do the 47-second prompt.

1. Get physically close. Stand next to him. Bend down and look directly into his eyes.
2. Place your hand in the center of his back. (With tactile defensive kids, place your hand on desk / work table.)
3. Whisper in a calm, soft voice in his ear, "Bill do your work." Use his name. Give a direct, positive command. This prompts him to get back on task. Your physical closeness will guarantee he'll begin to work.
4. Say nothing. This is the most difficult part. Remain close until you see him making an effort. This should take less than 30 seconds.
5. Then say, "Thank you, Bill."

The simple method works because you've responded to misbehavior with calm, not anger. You've reinforced and rewarded good behavior. The closeness insures the student will get back on task. A "craving for attention" child receives physical comfort. You've established a positive, caring feeling between you and your student.

# Students Respond

Students respond with, "You are welcome," Mrs. Fuery. Warning: if you have eight kids not doing their work, tearing around the room or punching each other, this method will fail. (Try another technique.) This works if you have one or two students off task.

## 8. Sweet and sour strategy

A student will more likely hear you if you approach him/her first with a positive statement. The Sweet and Sour Strategy gets kids to listen. Here's an example:

I observed Jennifer, a fifth grader, enter the room and punch another student, Randy, on the shoulder. She's now seated. I move close to her and say:

"Jennifer, I really like that yellow blouse you're wearing today. That color looks good with your dark hair. However, I didn't like what I saw just a few moments ago. You punched Larry on the way into class. I know for the rest of this hour, you'll do the right thing and keep your hands to yourself." Follow this with a handshake or a pat on the shoulder. Walk away. Turn your attention to someone else.

If you continue to stand near Jennifer, she may justify her behavior. You've said what's needed. Don't belabor your point or you'll lose the power of the Sweet and Sour approach.

## 9. The Simple Scolding

The Simple Scolding can be done after a class or after a misbehavior has occurred. Basically, you're letting the youngster know how you feel.

When I meet with a student at the end of class it gives me an edge. I have calmed my emotions. I plan what I'll say. Privacy is important. The rest of the class doesn't need to hear my words.

When the entire class can watch like spectators, it's best not to confront an angry student. Why? Because the student becomes the performer and you're the show.

## The Gatsby Incident

We were watching the movie, *The Great Gatsby.* One scene involved a man slugging a woman in the mouth. Right after this scene, several students laughed. I turned off the projector and confronted their behavior.

I asked if they felt laughter was an appropriate response. We discussed the scene briefly, then the projector went back on.

One student, Bryan, who often disrupted the class with his outbursts, sat in the back of the room. He continued to laugh almost out of control. Since there was another teacher in the classroom, I could pull Bryan aside. Quietly, I asked him to follow me.

### The Simple Scolding In Action

We went next door to an empty classroom. Leaving the door open, I pulled up two chairs and motioned him to be seated. I looked into his eyes with a sad expression. I said:

"Bryan, I can't predict your emotional reaction to any scene. I feel bad when you laugh after the class is settled down. It disturbs me to see you laugh at another person's pain. Even though this is a movie, it disturbs me. That's how I feel. You're an intelligent and sensitive young man. I know in the future, I can count on you to do what's right. Thank you for talking with me."

The Simple Scolding uses "I" messages. It's a positive approach that brings results. The teacher is calm and rational and says with his/her behavior, "I'm in charge. I'm in control of my feelings."

Limit your criticism to only one misbehavior. Keep the scolding short. Always give the student a sincere compliment and always thank the student.

If Bryan had said, "But Mrs. Fuery....it was George's fault." My response would be, "Bryan, this is not a conversation we're having. Please listen."

You don't want an explanation for inappropriate behavior. You're not blaming him, so he has no reason to justify his actions. The Simple Scolding works because students leave with their dignity and self-respect intact.

# Chill Out Areas
## 1. The rocking chair

Because of my strong Southern heritage, I believe in the benefits of rocking chairs. Rocking chairs were in my grandmother's kitchen in Dublin, Georgia. And the moments I spent in an old wooden rocker sipping iced tea on the wrap-around porch are precious to me.

It's hard to chill out in Georgia in July, but that is exactly what I did sitting in those rocking chairs. Kids today need rockers, too. I have a white pine rocking chair in my classroom. It cost me 20 bucks at a garage sale, and it has been a discipline bargain. Because my classroom has no windows, the chair is located in a back corner next to a sunset beach poster. It's amazing how well it works to cool aggression.

My high school students arrive early to rock before the bell rings. If the chair is occupied, they sit on the floor. A rocker relieves tension and stress, gives comfort and movement and is drug-free. What more could we ask?

## Rocking Chair Uses

When I ask a student to stay after the bell for a few minutes (for the Simple Scolding) I always direct him/her to the rocker. I gauge the student's emotional state by how fast the rocker moves.

## Active Kids

If I had to sit for six hours or stay the entire day in one room, I'd probably lose my mind. Why? I'm extremely active. It's a great advantage while teaching and giving seminars, but a real detriment when trying to write at a computer or sit still for longer that 45 minutes.

When I'm asked to give an all-day seminar, one of the most common responses I hear from teachers is, "I loved what I was learning, but I hated having to sit all day long."

Sitting all day is tough on teachers as well as on students. That's why we have frequent stretch and bathroom breaks. When I teach all-day seminars, the afternoon session involves group work and lots of movement. Both adults and kids need the chance for physical movement. Physical movement needs to be part of the lesson plan.

## 2. Thinking chairs

To allow for physical activity, keep two or three "thinking" chairs on the sides or back of the room. Thinking chairs are not punishment chairs. They help students monitor their own behavior. Students ask for permission to go to a thinking chair. Or, in my classroom, a student may sit in a thinking chair, if he/she feels staying at their desk or table will get him/her in trouble.

I was recently discussing the use of thinking chairs with a seventh grade teacher. She said, "Those chairs won't work in my classroom. My students are way too immature to know when to move away from trouble." We need to teach when to move away from trouble as an essential skill.

## 3. Personal office

One elementary teacher had an extremely active, emotionally handicapped girl named Linda. She was mainstreamed into her second grade class. The teacher created an "office" for this out-of-control student.

The teacher unscrewed the legs on a study carrel. Linda sits on the floor and slides her legs under the bottom of the desk. It's the one time all day she's not moving. The study carrel acts as a constraint. She is better behaved and more on task in her "little office" than anywhere else in the room.

Study carrels work with all levels of students. They are cozy and secure. One year I had a tough group of high school seniors. The class contained all boys who had failed English two or three times. Eighteen of these young people were jammed into a small classroom.

The only thing that saved my sanity was the row of six study carrels, where I isolated a few of them each day. As long as the instigators were on task in their little space, the rest of the group functioned fine.

## 4. Area Rugs/Rug Squares

Washable rugs and rug squares can create a clean floor space for stretching, moving, reading or working on the floor in groups and reading. Just as arranging space helps ease tension and create harmony in a classroom, so does providing outlets for aggressive behavior. We need to deflate the aggression and stop being the student's target.

# Outlets for Aggression

## 1. Soft objects

Punching bags, soccer boppers, soft bats, pillows.

## 2. Swearing box

Especially popular with the elementary set, the Swearing Box is a small box made of construction paper. Ask an art teacher to show you how to make one. An angry student writes lots of swear words on pieces of paper and puts them into the box. Words are written on the outside of the box. Collect and use shoe boxes for this purpose.

## Up-Beat Talks: The Start Up

"It's good to see that you've read the assignment on the board. I'm glad you have your books open and your paper out. Your desk looks prepared, Dee, Shelly and Dick, thank you. You're ready to start class."

## Leave Your Troubles

"I hope you left your troubles in that imaginary book bag outside the classroom door. You don't need them. This is a place where you're safe. You can be happy here. You can pick up that book bag again when you leave, if you still want to carry it with you."

## The Bell Quiz

There's no better way to get a group of kids focused, than to begin each class with a brief, five question quiz. The questions cover the homework or the work from the day before.

As the bell rings, the teacher says, "Thank you for being ready to begin today's quiz. Number one ..."

## The Five-Minute Miracle

The bell quiz is a short miracle. Ask questions out loud. Short answers make grading swift. Students trade papers and grade the test in class. Papers are then collected or handed over to a specific student to be put in alphabetical order.

Save paper by putting each week's quizzes on one sheet of notebook paper. Spread out papers you are returning on a desk near the door. As students enter the classroom, they pick up their quiz sheet.

# Improve Discipline

When they don't have enough to do, kids get into trouble. The quiz gives kids worthwhile work, reviews the previous lesson and gets students quiet immediately. It starts the class with a jolt.

If kids are late, they miss the quiz. There is no make-up. If they enter late with a legitimate pass, or if they have an excused absence, put O.K. next to their name in grade book. If they have an unexcused absence they get a zero. Three zeroes equal one afternoon detention with the teacher.

# Summary

**47-Second Prompt**

1. Get close.
2. Place hand on desk.
3. Whisper command.
4. Keep silent.
5. Thank student.

**The Simple Scolding**

1. Tell the student how you feel.
2. State the misbehavior. Be brief. Wait. Stare. Let the student feel your sincere unhappiness.
3. Give the student sincere encouragement or a compliment.
4. Thank student. Use his/her name.

**Fix Brush Fires**

1. Use eye contact. Actively listen.
2. Get close. Use a strong voice.
3. Try the sweet/sour approach.
4. Use a rocking chair/thinking chairs.
5. Create isolated offices.
6. Find outlets for aggression.

# 8

# *Boundary Setting for*
# *Ballistic Kids*

Students crave boundaries. They need to know what's acceptable and unacceptable in your classroom. Before you enforce rules, kids need to know what the rules are.

Some teachers give rules the first day of school and never mention them again. Effective teachers remind students often of the parameters they've established.

Classroom behavior is set within the first two weeks of school. The first week, make sure your rules are understood. Before any new activity, give reminders. Situations change. Regularly update students on correct behavior.

## Classroom Rules

1. **Everyone deserves respect.**
2. **Come to class prepared.**
3. **Have a winning attitude.**
4. **Do your best.**
5. **Do what's right.**

# Rule 1: Everyone deserves respect

"I respect myself as your teacher, and I respect you as my students. I feel the teacher/student relationship is important. It lasts a lifetime. I'm grateful to be a successful teacher. I like what I do. I like coming to school. You're important to me. I have a high regard for myself. I also have a high regard for you.

"During class discussions, I'll ask you to share your feelings and beliefs. I respect your right to hold a different opinion from mine. I may not agree. However, I'll support your freedom to express your thoughts. I won't belittle you. I won't allow another student in this class to make cutting remarks toward me or you.

"We are a support group and a team. Some of your best friends will come from here. Do you know everyone?

"Several years ago, a student wrote, 'I didn't believe that crap about finding my best friends in this class. Rick and I will be roommates next year at the University of Florida. All the work you made us do as teams is the cause.'

"By the end of the year, you'll have made some of your strongest supporters and closest friends right from this class."

# Rule 2: Come to class prepared

"When the bell rings, have a prepared desk. That means you need pencils, a pen and paper on your desk. Have your book open to the page number listed on the board.

"I'll list the day's activities on an overhead projector or the board. This information can be found in the same place each day.

"As you entered, did you notice the table next to the door? That table is most important. Your class notebooks, graded papers, textbooks, daily quiz paper and all make-up work are located there. As you enter, read the daily assignment, pick up what you need from the table and get your desk prepared. When the bell rings, work begins."

## Rule 3: Have a winning attitude

"You decide if this is a good or bad day.

"Let's say you woke up this morning in a cheerful mood. You felt great. You decided to wear your favorite blue denim shirt. It wasn't pressed. You pulled on a tan shirt that you didn't like. Next, as you sat down for breakfast, you poured milk on your cereal. It smelled terrible because it had spoiled. You decided to eat yogurt."

"You arrive tardy to class, rush into your room and sit next to your buddy, Aaron. He says, 'You look like a sick turkey in that shirt.' Here's the important part.

"You choose. You can let the disappointment of spoiled milk, getting a tardy and hearing a friend's insult all defeat you. Or you can decide — There have been a few bad moments this morning, but I'm handling this. I'm still in a good mood.

"A winning attitude helps you rise above disappointments.

"A winning attitude says, 'I'm strong. I decide to be happy.' A losing attitude says, 'I can't.' When you come into this room, put on your good face and say to yourself, 'I think I can.'

"Bad things happen to good people all the time. We control our reaction to events in our lives. When we decide to have a winning attitude, moods are under our control."

## Rule 4: Do your best

"I promise as your teacher to do my best. I ask that you give your best, too. Your papers may not always earn an 'A', but your best is the best. Mistakes are O.K.

"Sometimes when I'm teaching or writing, I ask myself, 'Am I doing my best? ' Sometimes the answer is, 'No.' Then I ask myself, 'What can I do to do my best?' Usually there's something I can do to improve. Reminding myself to do my best helps me. I know it will help you, too."

## Rule 5: Do what's right

"This is my favorite rule. When I fail to do what is right, then I make mistakes. The following story illustrates something that happened to me in the eighth grade. It shows what occurs when the last two rules aren't followed.

## Green Garment Nightmare

"Mrs. Pluckett was my eighth grade home economics teacher. We began the school year with cooking. Our first recipe was tomato aspic

"I don't remember the recipe, but I do remember my first silly, dirty joke. Another girl told it to me over

**89**

the sink. I can't repeat it now except under the influence of sodium penathol. But jokes and cooking didn't get me into nearly the hot water that sewing did. That was my nemesis.

"Mrs. Pluckett picked out what appeared to be an easy pattern. The sack dress a sleeveless design with drawstring waist. By the time I finished, the dress belonged on a bag lady.

"My mother selected a putrid green fabric. It was a nightmare. The pinning, the cutting, the sewing. I'm sure this Chatty Cathy was given plenty of class time to complete the project. Instead of sewing, I spent hours talking with friends. I also spent hours standing outside the classroom door, as a punishment for terrorizing Mrs. Pluckett.

"Days before the dress was due, I smuggled it home for my mother to complete. My sack dress made so many trips home, it deserved frequent flyer points. I didn't realize a nark lurked in the classroom.

"My mother wasn't a good seamstress either. Unfortunately, I found out too late. The day before the big grading and display of our sewing talents, legally we were to take our masterpieces home to wash, starch and press to perfection.

"All the proper, behaving girls took their dresses home for the final primping, plumping and pressing. My poor mother was pushed to the limits of her talents. She barely completed the dress. Forget washing, forget starching and forget pressing.

"Grading day arrived. Mother earned me a distinction — the only 'F' dress in the class. Mrs. Pluckett knew about my clandestine operations. But that wasn't the worst news. The worst news was that I had to wear my 'F' dress to class the next day.

"I think Mother deserved a 'D' maybe even a 'D+'. What'd ya' say, Mrs. Pluckett?

"Did I earn the grade? Did Mrs. Pluckett hate me? I wasn't doing my best and I wasn't doing what was right."

# Making Rules Work

## 1. Kids buy into them

A dog food company held its annual sales convention. The president listened patiently as her advertising chief produced a campaign guaranteed to push up profits. Then the marketing head extolled the virtues of his department. Next, the sales director described the incredible sales team. Finally, the president closed with a speech.

"Over this entire day," she began, "I've heard about our wonderful plans for the new year. But I still have one question. If we have the best advertising campaign going, the most creative marketing people in the country and the most talented sales force, then why do we sell less damn dog food than any other company in the business?"

The convention room was silent. Finally, a small voice answered from the back of the room, "Because the dogs hate it."

If dogs don't like the dog food, you won't sell much. If students don't agree to the merits of a rule, you won't get too many followers. One way to get kids to buy into a rule is to have them write one or two. Then vote and add to your list.

Remember to keep the total number of rules to five, otherwise you'll have trouble remembering them.

## 2. Rules are like icebergs

Good rules are like icebergs because they go beyond the surface. They represent unspoken and unexpressed behaviors.

About three weeks into a new school year, I ask my students to list behaviors that are not allowed in the classroom.

One student wrote, "Talking while the teacher is talking." Another expressed, "Cutting others down." These thoughts weren't specific rules, but show how good rules become guidelines for correct behavior.

## 3. Keep rules positive and general

"Do what's right," and "Do your best," are positive, general and easy to remember.

If you have rules that begin with, "Don't," you reiterate a negative behavior. If you tell students, "Don't set milk cartons on fire," your students think, "What fun. I hadn't thought of that before."

Remind students often that the locus or the center of control is in their power. Students tell me, "I can't help being in a bad mood." Give students the skills to cope with unpleasant events. They'll learn they can enjoy a good day, even when unpleasant events occur.

## 4. Rules apply to teachers

The classroom lacks privacy. Teachers are on stage and kids watch our every move. We're role models.

Most schools have rules about eating and drinking in the classrooms. If we don't want students consuming sodas in class, then we need to drink our coffee in the teachers' workroom, not the classroom.

Remember the old adage, "What you're doing is shouting so loudly that I can't hear what you're saying." We model our rules everyday. Through our comments about the school, our colleagues, the principal and our teaching, we speak volumes. We express ourselves with our clothes, body language, physical appearance and facial expressions.

## 5. Give frequent reminders

When teachers assume that kids know proper behavior, they make a big mistake. Airlines don't assume adults know how to buckle a seat belt.

When you board a plane, a stewardess welcomes you over the microphone. She asks that you pay attention to five minutes of safety tips. She doesn't assume you have learned or remember how to buckle a seat belt, so she tells you. Using matter-of-fact terms she explains in a positive, upbeat style.

Airline companies begin every flight the same way — with safety tips. We can begin each new activity the same way — with a quick reminder of the rules.

## Irrational Student Thoughts
**Everyone at school has to like me.**
**I must be good at everything I do.**
**My friends made me do it.**
**You made me feel this way.**
**It's all your fault.**
**I can fix your problems.**
**There's only one right way to do things.**
**I feel so bad, I wish I could die.**
**The whole school was laughing at me.**
**I'll never be enough.**

An awareness of irrational beliefs is one way we equip kids to build their self-esteem. Regardless of what's happening in their external world, students need to control their inner voice. Getting students to recognize these irrational thoughts, is a big step in the right direction.

## 7. Teachers can't fix low self-esteem

A child isn't a fix-it-up project or a handyman's special. One teacher remarked about a female student, "I wish I knew how to make her feel better about herself. Perhaps more praise would have build her self-esteem."

Do you recall a time when someone tried to "plaster you with praise?" Did if feel good? Most likely the praise was false, and you resented the person giving the flattery. Kids are smart. They recognize a con job.

An excellent source for building self-esteem is the small, classroom paperback, *Thinking, Changing, Rearranging — Improving Self-Esteem In Young People* by Jill Anderson, Timberline Press, Inc., Box 70187, Eugene, OR 97401.

## 8. Average is good enough

We hear average isn't good enough. We are caught up in the neurotic need to be perfect. We don't want an average grade, an average day or an average car. We desire a top grade, an exciting job and a sporty car.

Garrison Keillor, radio personality and author, spoke about the fictitious Midwest town of Lake Wobegon. He always ended his radio shows describing Lake Wobegon with the words, "where all the children are above average."

It insults some parents to hear their child is average, but there's nothing wrong with being average. Parents want children who are *"gifted."* Yet all children have moments of *"giftedness."* And aren't all children a gift?

Students with average grades succeed. I was a 'C' student. Yet I was able to become successful and write books. I was blissfully ignorant. No one told me a 'C' student couldn't achieve, so I did.

A friend of mine referred respectfully once to her son as a "gentlemanly 'C' student." That was much more acceptable than saying, "My son is just average." His grades were totally insignificant when, at the age of 16, he was killed in a car crash. When we tell students that a 'C' grade is not good enough, we need to be aware of our message.

## Summary

**Classroom Rules**
1. Everyone deserves respect.
2. Come to class prepared.
3. Have a winning attitude.
4. Do your best.
5. Do what's right.

**Boundary Setting**
1. Get kids to buy into the rules.
2. Rules apply to teachers and students.
3. Give frequent reminders.
4. The locus of control is in our power.
5. Explain irrational thoughts.
6. A child is not a handyman's special.
7. Teacher's can't fix low self-esteem.
8. Average is good enough.

# 9

# *Target Your Anger And Help Kids Manage Theirs*

During my first year of teaching, I wore a tough shield for protection. I wasn't human, and this facade wasn't me.

One morning before homeroom, two students greeted me with the Nazi stance and a "Heil, Hitler." That gives you some indication of my personality. There was power in my emotional tirades, but the price I paid was too high.

## Do You Avoid Confrontation?

Because getting angry carries an emotional cost, we sometimes do the opposite. We avoid confrontation. We'd rather comply than confront. We ask ourselves, "How can I please students? How can I win love and approval? How can I keep the peace?" Instead, we need to ask, "What behavior is appropriate in my classroom? What behaviors will I tolerate? What behaviors will I not tolerate?"

If we fail to clarify what's acceptable student behavior, then we devalue ourselves. Students pick up quickly on our weakness. Anger that's unconsciously denied is transformed into guilt, confusion, and pain such as headaches and backaches.

# Natural Caregivers

Teachers are natural caregivers. We protect, help, nurture and comfort students. Anger occurs when we attempt to direct behaviors not in our control. When we're in the dance of anger, it's difficult to identify the moves.

We can take a firm stand, let go of blaming students for our unhappiness and target our anger. Here's how.

# Target Your Anger

## 1. Become the omnipotent observer

When you're angry, step outside yourself and observe the interaction. Instead of blindly reacting, ask yourself, "What's going on here?"

## 2. Talk with colleagues

Watch the way colleagues manage their anger. Discuss with other teachers effective ways to manage misbehaving kids.

## 3. Be aware of subconscious anger

Our anger finds expression in passive-aggressive ways. Through body language and voice tone, we let students know that we don't like them. One year, I had a sixth-hour, ninth grade class that gave me prematurely gray hair. I realized that during the first weeks of school, I had allowed problems to escalate by tolerating inappropriate behaviors.

The next year, I was determined to be more firm. Instead I was overly harsh and angry. About the second week of school, a brave senior not only picked up on my attitude, but approached me.

Lisa came up to my desk and asked, "You really don't like our class, do you? I'm wondering what we have done to make you so mean?"

She was sincere. I explained that the year before I had mismanaged my previous sixth hour class. I told her that I may have overreacted, and promised to make an effort to change my approach.

Lisa helped me realize I had unfairly compared one group of students to another. Confronting my pent-up anger and tempering it worked ... I made an effort to be more authentic with my feelings and that sixth hour group of seniors turned out to be one of the best I have ever taught.

## 4. Before confrontations, consider:

What makes me angry?
What's the real issue ?
Where do I stand?

## 5. Avoid teacher talk

Teacher talk phrases include:
"Buckle down."
"Behave yourself."
"Shape up."
"Stop that."

Belittling tactics are equally ineffective and include: labeling, preaching, ordering, warning, ridiculing and lecturing. Kids tune us out.

## 6. Use the student conference

When you confront a child in front of the class, other students become attorneys. Keep confrontations short. I like to retreat to the back of the classroom. I set up two chairs — a rocking chair and a straight chair. The straight chair is for me. I pull it up close so that we are looking eye to eye.

The student conference isn't a conversation. It's a one-to-two minute reprimand that lets the young person know that you're unhappy with the misbehavior. It releases anger in a constructive way.

Decide in advance what behavior you'll reprimand. Reprimand one misbehavior per conference. Two chairs pulled close together at the back of the classroom creates the semi-private setting.

### Step 1 — State the way you feel

"I feel angry (frustrated, sad, hurt, disappointed, etc.) when you..."

### Step 2 — State the misbehavior

Use simple terms. Be direct.

### Step 3 — Wait

Look directly at the student. Match your facial expression to your mood. Silently count 15 seconds to let the student feel your emotions.

### Step 4 — Expect it not to recur

End with a closing, positive statement. Continue with, "Now that you know how I feel, I'm sure your behavior will improve. I like your work, talents, humor, insights, etc." Always end with a sincere compliment.

### Step 5 — Thank the student
Use his/her name. "Jennifer, I appreciate your staying after school. Thank you."
This two-minute conference works because my anger is directed. I'm calm. I'm not criticizing or berating, but sharing sincere feelings. It's amazing how good I feel after the student conference.

## 7. The 60-second time-out
From high school seniors to second graders, the 60-Second Time-Out saves your sanity. When a student has behaved inappropriately, call him/her back to your desk. Here are the various ways to use this technique.

### Elementary Level
Ask the student to count to 60 while holding your hand. Or, have the student watch the second hand on the clock. The hand-holding is especially effective with the younger set — kindergarten through third grade. Another way to use this method is to explain that the student cannot return to the group until he/she comes up with three better choices for the inappropriate behavior.

### Secondary Level
**Option 1:** Missing one minute of lunchtime or staying after class one minute works miracles to

correct behavior of middle and high school students. Ask the student to come up with three better choices for his/her behavior. **Option 2:** Tell your student, "I see you've decided to break a class rule. Tell me what rule you broke and what alternative behavior would have been more appropriate." **Option 3:** Tell your student, "You have a choice here. I see you chose to break rule number three which is, 'Do what's right.' What better choices could you make in the future?"

## 8. Avoid toxic teacher areas

Faculty lounges as well as teacher work areas can be poisoned with negativity and gossip. Steer clear of these toxic dump sites. Negative comments don't help resolve problems. Gossip is destructive and a passive way of dealing with conflict. Consider yourself a guilty party if you're the one encouraging the perpetrator with the words, "Oh, tell me more."

## 9. Use self-talk

Effectively targeting anger and learning alternative methods for maintaining composure is made easier with encouraging self-talk. The following more specific reinforcements are useful.

## Step 1 — Prepare for conflict

"This may be rough, but I can handle it. I'm in control. I'm calm and I'll stick to the issues and not take anything personally. I won't argue. I know what to say and do."

## Step 2 — Cope with physical response

"My body signals what I need to do. I'll take a deep breath and relax my muscles. I'm calm and dealing with this conflict constructively."

## Step 3 — During confrontation

"I'm in control and handling this situation. My voice is calm and quiet. I'm in charge. I can do it."

## Step 4 — After confrontation

**Conflict resolved**:

"I'm proud of myself. I kept cool and collected. I stated my feelings without attacking, raising my voice or getting angry. I'm doing better at this. I knew I could do it."

**Unresolved conflict**:

"I can now relax. I won't take this personally. I did my best. I'll reward myself today by thinking about something else. Tomorrow is a new day to work out a solution."

## 10. Use reflective listening

When we feel we aren't being heard, both teachers and students get angry. Reflective listening is a way to resolve conflict in all our relationships. We can use this method with kids and can teach our students to use this technique with others in the classroom. It is similar to the mirroring technique used in chapter six, *"Games Kids Play."*

## Set-Up

1. Sit knee to knee.
2. Set a timer to ring in ten minutes.
3. One student is the "speaker"; the other student is the "listener."
4. The speaker gets a piece of linoleum. This means he/she has the floor.
5. The speaker states feelings in clear, short phrases.
6. The listener re-states, paraphrases feelings back to the listener.
7. After ten minutes, the timer rings. Students change places.

## Reflective Listening Rules

**No zings**

This means no cut-downs or put-downs. A zing is considered a zing if it hurts the feelings of the listener.

**Watch body language/voice tone**

**To speakers**: Keep your voice calm. Speak slowly. Pause often to let the listener re-phrase your words.

**To listeners**: Lean forward, give eye contact, show interest by giving attention and focusing thoughts on the speaker.

## 11. Manage student anger

Many schools have set up "time-out" areas where kids who continually disturb the class can go. In Florida, where over-crowded classes are the norm, many schools don't have the space for a time-out room. An alternative is to have a desk designed as the time-out area.

Another solution is to send the student to another teacher's classroom, preferably one where the disrupting student does not know lots of other kids.

When I taught middle school, I sent eighth graders into sixth grade classes. I made prior arrangements with the sixth grade teacher. When my student appeared at the other teacher's doorway, a desk was made available. As soon as the student had filled out either the Squabble Sheet or the Time-Out Report, the student could return to my classroom. You will find a copy of each form at the close of this chapter.

Why did this method work? Because I had a chance to get the class settled down and working without a disruptive influence. The misbehaving student had a chance to cool down and reflect on what had occurred. I found my own solution and didn't have to involve an administrator in the problem.

The two discipline forms that follow can be used in your classroom. Pick one that works best for you.

## Summary

1. Target your anger.
   Talk with colleagues.
   Be aware of teacher talk.
2. Use student conference.
3. Use 60-second time-out.
4. Avoid toxic teacher areas.
5. Use self-talk for conflict resolution:
   Prepare, cope, confront and reflect.
6. Try reflective listening.
7. Use squabble sheets/time-out reports.

# Squabble Sheet

Name:_____ Date_____

Where was I? Check one.

☐ Classroom     ☐ Bathroom          ☐ Cafeteria
☐ Office        ☐ Gym               ☐ Other_____

What happened? Check one.

☐ I was insulted        ☐ I was robbed
☐ I was attacked        ☐ Verbally?     ☐ Physically?
☐ I did something wrong...      ☐ Other _____

Write a brief paragraph describing what happened.

_____

_____

_____

_____

Who caused the problem? Check one.

☐ myself        ☐ another student       ☐ an adult
☐ other _____

How did I respond? Check one or more.

☐ Hit back          ☐ Told an adult         ☐ Ran away
☐ Yelled            ☐ Cried                 ☐ Talked it out
☐ Broke something                           ☐ Ignored it
☐ Was restrained    ☐ Used self-talk to control my anger

How did I handle myself? Circle one.

1-Poorly   2-Okay   3-Well   4-Wonderfully

How angry was I?

☐ not angry         ☐ angry but in control
☐ very angry        ☐ furious and steaming

What can your teacher do about this problem?

_____

_____

What can I do about my problem?

_____

_____

**107**

# Time-Out Report

Name:_____ Date:_____

I was asked to leave _____'s classroom and fill out this paper. Here is my account of the events that led to my leaving the room.

Did I stop the teaching in the classroom?

Explain._____

Were other students distracted by what I did?

_____

Put a circle around one of the questions that best relates to your mood at the time of the incident:

☐ I wanted to get even with someone.

☐ I wanted to get revenge.

☐ I wanted to feel superior to someone.

☐ I wanted to hurt someone.

If you can't answer any of the above questions with a "Yes" then write your own statement that best shows your mood. I wanted to .

Put a check in front of the following questions that relate to your situation. Answer the appropriate questions.

☐ Did someone get hurt?

☐ Was something broken or damaged?

☐ Was someone embarrassed?

☐ Did I waste my time?

☐ Did I waste the teacher's time? How?

_____

☐ What did I lose? _____

☐ What did I gain? _____

What positive thing could the teacher do to help us get along better?_____

_____

What positive thing could I do to help myself?_____

_____

_____

# 10

## *Soothe Ballistic Behaviors*

**D**iscipline problems in schools follow the 80/20 rule — 80 percent of all discipline problems occur with 20 percent of the students. This 20 percent has the ability to create havoc and mayhem. It makes sense to find remedies for the ballistic behavior of one-fifth of our students.

### One Frustrated Cootie

When I was growing up, my three brothers gave me the nickname "Cootie". I was about seven years old when this name stuck like glue. Pointing a finger at me meant only one thing — I was a cootie.

Finger-pointing became my number one torment. I was an easy prey. My brothers were relentless — pointing at me during dinner, before I left for school, while we were watching TV and just about anytime they wished to be entertained by my reaction.

A finger sent me into hysterics. I was as well-trained as one of Pavlov's dogs.

I cried to my mother, "Jimmy's calling me 'Cootie.' "

"I didn't hear him say anything."

"He's not. He's pointing his finger at me."

"Jimmy, stop pointing at your sister."

In five minutes, pointing began again. It's a

wonder we didn't lose our sanity. I wish I'd known about the ignoring game while I was growing up.

## 1. The ignoring game

Select a student who doesn't get upset easily. Ask him/her to demonstrate with you. Tell the student that you'll be doing a variety of annoying behaviors. While ignoring you, the student continues working.

You've picked Rick. Stand close to him. Tug on his hair, step on his foot, pull at his jacket or shirt. Rick shouldn't respond. After two minutes, turn to the class and talk about what you've demonstrated.

## Explanation

"Class, the purpose of this activity is to show that inappropriate behaviors don't need an audience. When we respond to these actions with laughter, anger or any other emotion, we're rewarding the student who acts inappropriately. Unless the behavior is physically harmful, ignore this student."

After explaining this activity to sixth graders, one teacher, Craig Wilcox, had an interesting reaction. During an outburst, one girl turned to her classmates and said, "Let's play the ignoring game. Mr. Wilcox will give us bonus bucks." (Paper money used to buy privileges.)

Reward kids who are clever enough to ignore harmless behavior. Students trapped in the victim role, now have other options.

## 2. The comic

One of my sixth-hour high school students, Steve Ryan, was a terrific comedian. Because he disrupted class often, I came up with a survival technique. Promising to keep his remarks short, he began the period with a joke or humorous statement. Most of the time he was quite funny, took two minutes of class time and received the attention he needed in a positive way. We called these openings, "Ryanisms." On days when Steve had nothing to say, we missed his "Ryanisms."

## 3. The box

The Kid In The Box works well with elementary students. In the center of the room, draw an imaginary box around a desk. Tell the class if a student misbehaves, he/she will sit in the box (for a specific amount of time) to work.

While in the box, we can't hear or see this child. Elementary teachers agree that this method gives children lots of attention, but no strokes for misbehavior. Just like the ignoring game, we need the cooperation of the class to make it work.

## 4. Suspend disbelief

Samuel Coleridge wrote a poem called, "The Rime of the Ancient Mariner." In the introduction he explains to the reader that the poem contains supernatural elements. Coleridge asks his readers to "willingly suspend disbelief," and for the moment, to believe in the impossible. Believing in the impossible is what teachers do with students.

## 5. Let go of past hurts

Before the end of the day, resolve problems. Carrying hurts over and keeping score of wrongs works to defeat teachers. Like excess baggage, we need to leave the hurts behind.

Compliments get stuck in our throats about March. We need to bury the past and see each day as a brand new beginning. "Begin again," should be our March motto.

## 6. Holiday slumps

Teaching the day before a holiday, and the first day back from vacation is difficult. Motivate students as well as yourself by planning lessons designed to generate interest and enthusiasm.

### Plan activities

The three days prior to the Thanksgiving holiday, my high school seniors were unmotivated. To enhance this lackluster season and create concern, I made the deadline for oral reports, based on student research papers, due the Monday of that three-day week. The research paper was a two-person team project. Experts on their subjects, my students taught the class. I sat in the back of the room and graded the papers at the same time the students gave their oral reports. Attendance and attention were excellent. I enjoyed a stress-free holiday. The return to school was also easy because I used that day for make-up reports.

## 7. Pretend it's September

At the beginning of the school year we're nicer.

We remember "please" and "thank you." Something happens to our manners about the middle of February. We lose patience easily. We show irritation. One way to cope is to pretend it's September. With the entire year ahead, we treat students better.

### 8. Apologize — when it's not your fault

Airline personnel do this all the time. If there's bad weather, the pilot will make the announcement, "I'm sorry for the air turbulence. We'll resume cabin service shortly. Thank you for your patience." The pilot didn't create the weather and he/she doesn't have to apologize for it. What does an apology do? It softens the disappointment. It 's another way of saying, "I care."

### 9. Give sincere compliments

Offer meaningful approval. Sometime teachers come on too strongly with praise, then kids see compliments as insincere. It helps to keep the approval in line with the actual performance. Praise the achievement.

Make compliments calm, specific, sincere and to the point. Compliment expected behavior. Kids behave correctly much of the time. Give them credit.

Open a class with, "I appreciate your coming to school today. Thank you for having your books open to page 122, etc."

### 10. Refuse to label students

In a graduate class, a teacher of emotionally handicapped students gave a report. To make a point, she used one of her students as an example, and referred to her third-grader as "retarded." The professor corrected her twice.

When the teacher used the term a third time, the professor was clearly irritated. The woman defended herself. "Eight years ago, when I began teaching, I used the word, 'retarded'. It was accepted then."

"It's not acceptable now," responded the professor.

Calling a child, "retarded" labels that child. An expectation always follows. After the derogatory label is attached, our ability to see the good stops. A teacher who calls a child "retarded" closes doors on that child's abilities.

We misunderstand students when we don't expect good behavior and positive outcomes. It may be difficult for students to stay in school, behave appropriately and get work turned in, but it's much more difficult for them when we tell students they'll never straighten out their lives and that they're doomed.

> **Because of our expectations,**
> **students succeed or fail.**
> **Expectations shape lives.**

Not until the Israelites saw the Promised Land as an opportunity and as a chance to change their lives and create a new reality were they allowed to enter.

**115**

Believing in students creates a promised land and a hopeful, new reality.

## 11. Make smooth transitions

Very young children, active children, drug abusive kids and even some high school, "average" students don't make transitions easily. Identify the students who have difficulty with transitions. Then say, "In five minutes we will be switching from reading to writing."

Changes that are too sudden create discipline problems. Let kids know ahead of time what's coming up next.

**Suggestions for smooth transitions:**
Be physically close.
Get eye contact.
Place your hands on the student's elbow.
Check for understanding. Ask, "What are you doing next?"

## 12. Touch students

It was a Saturday morning in August. A cool breeze swept the street corner in downtown Minneapolis where I was waiting for a bus to take me to the Mall of America. Several women in a group stood close together, chilled by the breeze, but obviously excited about the upcoming shopping adventure.

With the women, were two young teenage girls. Both were dressed in cotton, short-sleeved shirts and jeans. One girl, about 13-years-old, stood with her

**116**

mother's arms wrapped tightly around her. Her companion looked over at the mother/daughter scene and remarked, "I wish I had my mom here to keep me warm."

Another lady in the group said, "Oh, come here. Any one of us would be delighted to warm you up." She put her arms around the smiling young girl.

Looking for the comfort, warmth and attention that touch brings, this youngster was brave and confident enough to ask for what she needed. She was lucky. She had an adult who recognized her request and filled her need.

About a month later, I was getting materials ready for my fifth-hour, ninth grade class. Three students arrived and were seated. Popular and attractive, Jason, walked into the room, looked at the girls and announced, "I need a hug." One girl obliged him.

## Starved For Touch

Most of our students aren't this brave. Too many don't know what they need, and if they do they are afraid to ask for it. They are starving for the human touch.

Physical contact is under siege. Let's get over the fears and relate to students through the power of touch. Before hugging a child, ask permission.

My high school students know that I won't touch them in a dark room, or keep just one student after school for detention.

Do you remember the *"60 Minutes"* segment several years ago wherein a college professor kissed kids on the cheek when they gave correct answers? I recall the college students' expressions — a mixture of embarrassment, pride and amusement. They loved the positive attention. My students are safe. I won't try to kiss them. I will touch them appropriately and with their permission.

## 13. Write magic cards

The magic card is an evaluation of the teacher and the class. Use magic cards to get helpful, positive feedback and to improve your teaching. Guide students by writing the following on the board or overhead:

**What do you like about this class?**
**What do you not like?**
**What could be improved?**

## Explaining Magic Cards

"Class, this is an individual assignment that takes about ten minutes. I've given each of you an index card. I call the index card a 'magic card' because it helps me change. The principal comes into this room twice a year to evaluate my teaching, but you're the ones who know me best. You're the experts. You're never asked.

"I'm asking now. I want your thoughts and feelings. I'm not concerned with handwriting or spelling. I'm looking for ways to improve as your teacher. I'm looking for honesty.

"I'm not perfect. The minute I become perfect, you'll be in trouble. Right now you're safe. You have the right to make mistakes and learn from those mistakes. I have that same right. I'm growing and becoming a better teacher. I need your help."

## After Instructions

Rather than collect the cards yourself, have students place them on a shelf. Do this activity on a day you're feeling good about yourself.

About four times a year, evaluate your teaching using magic cards. In May, the one, best question to ask is, "What did you enjoy most about this class?"

## 14. Try peer nominations

This is a technique for assessing a student's ability to get along with his/her classmates. If a child has difficulty relating to classmates, he/she will most likely have trouble relating to you. Peer nominations identify class leaders.

A child who is not selected may need some extra attention and help with social skills.

Ask the questions aloud, and have students write their answers. The following questions can be reworked for your teaching situation.

---

### Peer Nominations

**Who would you enjoy meeting for lunch?**
**Who would you pick as a partner?**
**Who would be your science project teammate?**

---

Well into the school year, a group of teachers conducted this survey. Some discovered students they had not considered as leaders. Even for those teachers who thought they knew their classes well, there were surprises. The negative aspects of this information is not to be shared with students.

## 15. Feed students

I took a graduate course to brush up on some new teaching techniques in the special education field. The class was made up of veteran teachers. Most of us worked full-time.

We met once a week for three hours at 4:30 p.m. During that first afternoon, we weren't a very enthusiastic bunch. The wise professor did two things that perked our interests.

First, she assigned two students each week to bring in snacks and finger food. At the end of a long teaching day, that late afternoon snack was a welcome treat. Second, she used the last four class sessions for team reports on specific areas of special-needs kids. We were responsible for the teaching.

The energy from the first meeting, with a lecture-style format, to the last classes, with "students" doing the teaching, was tremendous. Working as two-person teams, we took a personal interest in the one area in which we became "experts."

These two small changes in technique were responsible for the increase in energy, participation and enthusiasm. Feeding our faces and feeding our egos (by putting us in charge) were just two ways this aware, college teacher jumped-started our energy.

Using savvy remedies, good teachers divert disasters and solve discipline problems early. Show kids you care. Try something new and help eliminate the problems with our ballistic 20 percent.

## Summary

**Remedies for ballistic behavior:**

1. Play the ignoring game.
2. Give the comic the mike.
3. Place a kid in the box.
4. Suspend disbelief.
5. Let go of past hurts.
6. Anticipate seasons and slumps.
7. Pretend it's September.
8. Apologize — when it's not your fault.
9. Give sincere compliments.
10. Refuse to label kids.
11. Make smooth transitions.
12. With permission, touch kids.
13. Write magic cards.
14. Try Peer Nominations.
15. Feed students.

# 11

## *Manage The Main-Streamed*

**R**obert Frost, an American poet, once wrote, "Home is the place that when you go there, they have to take you in." School is the place that when children go there, teachers take them in regardless of the problems they bring to the task of learning.

## Is This Really a Problem?
Let's check to see if a problem exists. Before you attempt to direct a child's behavior, ask:
Is the behavior causing physical harm?
Is the behavior disrupting the learning?
Does the behavior create emotional reactions?
Is this child socially ostracized?

## Problem Prevention
### 1. Review the rules
Before an activity, prevent disruptive behaviors by reviewing the rules. Go over the rules by calling on students, or having the class recite the rules in unison. It's also important to review the consequences for disruptive behaviors.

## 2. Use humor

Bevil Lindsey, a veteran teacher, recommends that we sing a request to a child as a way to soften the impact and reduce tension. A child who is laughing is less likely to punch his/her classmate.

# ADD/ADHD

### Abbreviations:
Attention Deficit Hyperactivity Disorder = ADHD
Attention Deficit Disorder Without Hyperactivity=ADD

Attention Deficit Disorder, according to the *Merriam Webster's Collegiate Dictionary* is "a syndrome of learning and behavioral problems that is not caused by any serious underlying physical or mental disorder and is characterized by difficulty in sustaining attention, by impulsive behavior (as in speaking out of turn) and usually by excessive activity."

Have a peer teacher observe your classroom and the one child whom you feel needs special help. If the child has eight of the following characteristics, recommend to the parents that he/she be seen by a pediatrician.

## Characteristics ADD/ADHD:

Often fidgets with hands/feet and squirms in chair.
Student cannot remain seated.
Becomes easily distracted.
Waiting for turns in games, loses patience easily.
Easily excited and often blurts out answers.
Fails to complete assignments.
Difficulty staying focused on tasks or play.

Shifts from one uncompleted activity to another.
Experiences difficulty in playing quietly.
Interrupts frequently, excessive talker
Loses personal belongings.
Engages in physically dangerous activities.

## Where's My Secretary?

A student with ADHD and ADD can be compared according to Dr. Constance Clancy, a Florida mental health therapist, as "a busy business man or woman who does not have a secretary. The business person can't meet the deadlines or tend to all the details. As a result, the student does not complete assignments. He/she has difficulty with fine motor coordination which makes handwriting illegible."

## Is This a Speeding Car?

ADHD and ADD kids are often like speeding cars without brakes and steering. They are unable to control the direction of their behavior. If oral directions involve more than two or three steps, these student have trouble following them.

## Social Side Effects

Such children are untiring, creative, zestful, reckless and impulsive. They have problems in structured play where concentration is required. Not all adults who work with children understand the problems. One softball coach told a parent of an elementary-aged child with ADHD, "What your son needs is a good kick in the butt."

Another woman told me of her son's rejection by other kids in his fourth-grade classroom. Before he was on a good medical program, her son endured heartbreaking harassment. This child routinely checked his chair for tacks. Once his "meds" kicked in, it took over two years for his reputation to heal. His move to a larger, middle school, where the other kids didn't know his history, gave him a fresh start and new friendships.

## The Boys Have It

In the general population, three to five percent of the students have ADHD or ADD. The boys outnumber the girls by nine to one.

In conversations with elementary teachers I have discovered that many parents, especially fathers, oppose medication. The general attitude is, "How could anything be wrong with my son?"

## Deny the Problem?

Those of us who deny the problem exert much pressure on these kids to "act normal." When the child doesn't meet our expectations, then we become discouraged and anxious.

Teachers who put up with the behavior often vacillate between denial and acceptance. Our denial can lead to overly aggressive behavior directed at the student. Our acceptance may lead to lower expectations and inconsistent discipline.

The student senses our weakness and insecurity and either becomes confused or takes over control of the class.

## Handling the ADHD/ADD Child:

Realize that this student needs more structure, supervision and encouragement.

Spend additional time with this child.

Move away from windows and talkative kids.

When giving instructions, make eye contact. Sit close, ask the student to repeat to you what you expect him/her to do. Insist that this student maintains eye contact with you.

In addition to oral delivery, write instructions on an overhead or chalkboard.

If possible, have students type their papers.

Consistently remind this child to focus.

Show this student how you organize your work.

Have students work in teams of two.

Reward at short-term intervals. Give sincere praise for work completed.

When their medication is at its fullest potency, those youngsters are better behaved and more able to cooperate. When they're on the down side of their medication (before lunch or at the end of the day) give them tasks that don't require their full attention.

One side effect of Ritalin is a decrease in appetite. To offset this side effect, my elementary school colleagues recommend peanuts and peanut butter.

## Ritalin to the Rescue

Alice Baer, a veteran teacher, works with second graders at a private school in Florida. Two of the boys in her classroom were prescribed Ritalin by their pediatrician. They noticed the difference immediately in their class work, behavior and ability to concentrate.

A week later, one of the boys came up to her desk and suggested that another boy in the class needed Ritalin, too. This second grader even noticed the sharp improvement and felt medication might help his classmate.

Stephan Parker, a high school student who has learned to manage his ADHD, offered these suggestions: "Teachers need to give the student three assignments. Then they should say, 'Do this and I will give you something you want.' Now the student will say, 'Oh I can't do all three,' but the teacher must be firm."

In describing his feelings in elementary school (before his condition was diagnosed), he said, "I felt like I was stupid. Like all the other kids in class were better than me."

Now he takes medication and is doing average work. Stephan continued with, "This summer, I took algebra and the teacher and I got along. He suggested a tutor. The other kids in the class helped me, and I made a 95 on the final. If I can make a 95 on an algebra final, I can do anything. Now I feel like a knight in a chess game."

## Alternatives

Some parents are against providing drugs for ADD. Jim and Mimi Bailey of West Palm Beach, Florida, pulled their seventh grade son, Josh, out of public school. Mimi Bailey worked with Josh, who was diagnosed with ADD and dyslexia. She kept him in a home schooling program for almost two years.

When Josh went back to the ninth grade, he was offered the family car if he kept his grades up to a "C" average. By the time he graduated from high school, he maintained a "B" average and is now doing well in college.

Jim Bailey, reflecting on his son's progress said, "We were lucky. My wife has a degree in education. She stayed home with Josh. One of his problems with school was organizing his work into a small spaces. For example, with math problems, he needed lots of room for long division. He couldn't transfer correctly his answers to an answer sheet. Unfortunately, teachers were not willing to grade his papers individually.

"The system worked against him. Special education classes weren't the answer. Drugs were recommended but we vetoed that, too. We felt Josh needed time to resolve his problems himself. Keeping him in a home schooling program saved him." Because he wasn't hyperactive, teachers tended to overlook his problem.

## Drug Exposed Children

Prenatal substance exposed (PSE) children are those whose mothers used tobacco, alcohol, cocaine, crack, THC etc. while pregnant. About 11 percent of births in the United States are effected by alcohol and other drugs. In some minority populations, the rates are significantly higher. Within the native American population, 25 percent of all babies are reportedly damaged by alcohol.

Cocaine is more damaging to the infant than it is to the mother because it remains in the fluid surrounding the unborn infant for four to five days. About 20 percent of pregnant women in inner cities use crack and the numbers increase every year. In one Washington, D.C. hospital in 1988, one in ten babies were born with drug addiction. By 1991, that number increased to one in five.

Those children will learn the information but will have difficulty reaching what they've learned when they want to use it.

Keep in mind that almost all PSE children are in the normal range of I.Q. testing. Their problems aren't always the effects of the drug, but can stem from being raised by an addict or an inconsistent home environment. Because these children aren't easy to raise, many go from one foster home to another.

## Symptoms PSE Youngster:

Low motor skills — 90 percent-delayed language development.
Impulsive, hyperactive, and aggressive behavior.
Shy, quiet and overly withdrawn.
Uninhibited, irritable and jittery.
Easily distracted and frustrated.

These children's emotions are right on the edge. They can scream and be inconsolable one moment and be quiet and passive the next.

# Teachers Can . . .

The suggestions for handling children with ADHD/ADD works with PSE kids, too.

## 1. Give structure

At every moment, this child needs to know what to do and when to do it. Suggestions for structure include posting rules and schedules, drawing footprints to learning centers, etc.

## 2. Teach to one sense

The brightly colored posters and busy walls of the elementary classroom may put this child into stimulation overload.

## 3. Use soft lighting and pastel colors

Color and lighting helps control impulsive and aggressive behavior. The lighting should be iridescent, and the walls painted in muted shades.

## 4. Give affirmation

These children are hungry for affirmation. Don't assume that the child knows you like him/her. Make saying you like your students part of your daily routine. Students need to leave your classroom each day sensing, "My teacher really likes me."

## 5. Start each day with new hope

Our daily motto is, "Begin again." Clear the chalkboard of yesterday's problems. Begin each new day with renewed hope and fresh promise.

# External Threats

Poverty is a problem. The Center for the Study of Social Policy reports that one in every five children lives in an environment characterized by, "substandard housing, poor nutrition, high stress and inadequate health care." Part of this is due to the fact that 500,000 children are born to mothers who are themselves children under the age of 18.

Teachers cannot do much about poverty or poor health care but we can create an environment in our classroom where special-needs kids feel loved, accepted and appreciated. We must take them in and cherish their uniqueness.

## Summary

1. Review the rules.
2. Use humor.
3. Structure class time.
4. Sit close. Give your attention.
5. Ask students to repeat the directions.
6. Use short-term rewards.
7. Encourage pair work.
8. Teach to one sense at a time.
9. Have soft lighting and pastel walls.
10. Each new day, begin again.

# 12

## *Baby Bombers*
## *And Your Security*

Two bright 14-year old students who attended St. Coleman's Catholic School in Pompano Beach, Florida, broke into their classroom and planted a bomb they'd built from directions found on the Internet. The bomb came within five seconds of blowing up their teacher. The students called it a childhood prank. The state called it attempted murder. Their trial is pending.

Mae Groleau, the award-winning science teacher who switched on the classroom light, planned to work on the schools's yearbook. She noticed on the floor near her desk a broken fluorescent light bulb. The strong smell of gasoline fumes hit her and she snapped off the light.

If she had waited five seconds, bomb experts later testified, the explosion would have equaled 50 pounds of dynamite — enough dynamite to incinerate anyone in the classroom.

"It's very difficult," says Mae Groleau, "to walk into the classroom every day because you have to turn the light on ... you're thinking about what could've happened."

# One Band Teacher

I've lived in Lee County, Florida, for the last 21 years. In April, 1996, another shocking tragedy occurred. On Tuesday evening, a popular, 32-year-old teacher, Mark Schwebes, answered a 11:30 p.m. knock on his front door. A teenager shot him in the head.

Mark Schwebes, band leader at Riverdale High School, had spent the evening attending an ice cream social and recruiting incoming freshmen for the band. Pulling out of the parking lot, he noticed a few students hanging around the auditorium.

When Schwebes backed up his truck to see what the kids were up to, one boy who carried a can of gasoline, fled. Before Schwebes let the other boys go, he took gloves and some cans of food which they planned to use to break the auditorium's windows. He told the boys to expect a visit from the school's deputy.

Later that evening Schwebes related the incident to a parent. The parent recalled that the band leader wasn't overly concerned because one of the boys was a straight-A band student.

"He's got to die tonight. We're not going to jail," said the gang ringleader of the Lords of Chaos who the other members called, "God."

Hours later one gang member dialed directory assistance to get the band leader's home number. Over the telephone, they were given the teacher's home address. They called to make sure their teacher was home.

"It's ... a cruel irony that a teacher who was obviously a favorite among students to whom he had

133

dedicated his career and life," said Allen Caraway, spokesman for the Lee County School District.

## Tribute to Schwebes

A few days after the Schwebes murder, Paul A. Bernicchi, a former student from Port Charlotte, Florida, wrote a tribute to the band leader which was published in the editorial section of the Fort Myers News-Press, May 11, 1996.

"I was one of Mark Schwebes first students ... He was not always the 'good guy' among his students, but his arrival at Charlotte High School was a turning point in my music education ... He got me, his first chair trumpet player, thinking about my future and my potential.

"Four years later I am 30 credits away from a music education degree at Florida Southern College. I dedicate my senior year to the memory of Mark Schwebes ... It's really sad that it takes a tragedy for people to realize what a tremendous impact band directors like Schwebes have on ... children."

## What's Happening?

Atlanta psychologist Elizabeth Ellis, author of *Raising a Responsible Child* says, "What I see in teenagers these days is an incredible self-centeredness that boggles the mind ... Their biggest focus is how to get their needs gratified and when they don't get their needs gratified, they feel they have the right to be angry. And angry children act out, rebel and commit crimes."

"The child's sense of compassion ... seems to disappear between middle school and high school," adds Ellis. It isn't cool to want to save the whales or learn to play the French horn, but it's cool to build a bomb or brandish a firearm.

## The Awareness Factor

I'm not relating these two incidents to frighten you but rather to make you aware that bad things do happen to good teachers. Teachers have to be responsible for their own protection. We can't put the burden of our safety on the shoulders of a principal or school district.

For your personal and school protection, here are some precautions.

## 1. A non-published phone number

For a small monthly service, you can get a non-published number. Give your telephone number only to people you know and trust. Provide students and parents with your school telephone and fax line. Remember that unless you have a non-published number, directory assistance *does* give out your phone number and sometimes your address.

**Important reminder:** Caller I.D. units will list your number. To prevent this and protect yourself, press *67 before you dial. Check with your local phone carrier for specific details.

## 2. Don't put full name on mailbox

This along with your non-published address will make it difficult for a disgruntled student to find you.

### 3. Buy a mobile phone

Keep it with you at all times, both in your car and in your classroom.

### 4. When you work late notify the office

Tell one person you'll be staying late, then lock your classroom door.

### 5. Be aware in isolated parking lots

Especially before and after school, use caution in the parking lot. If you arrive early, wait a few moments in your locked car until someone else drives up. Walk into the building together. There is safety in numbers.

**If it's after normal school hours, ask someone to escort you from the school building to the parking lot.** If you head for the parking lot after dark, don't hesitate to ask a custodian to walk you to your car.

**Walk to your car with at least one arm free.** Have keys ready to unlock the door. Once inside, immediately lock all doors.

**Make eye contact with strangers.** If you see a stranger in the parking lot act confident. Give eye contact and greet the person. This behavior announces, "I've seen you. I can identify you."

### 6. Have a school-wide emergency signal

Have an emergency code word or phrase that can be used when calling the office so that you don't tip-off the students that you're signaling for assistance.

## 7. Don't carry open containers

Carrying your coffee cup, soda and bottled water into the classroom isn't a good idea. Make sure any container is sealed and kept in a locked place. One student in a New Jersey elementary school laced the teachers coffee with rat poison. Other students witnessed and reported the incident. It *can* happen to you.

## 8. Don't accept unwrapped food

I was handed an apple from three middle school students. It looked normal until the third bite — I discovered three embedded pennies.

## 9. Report suspicious activities

It doesn't matter where the activity occurs. Report any incidences immediately to your principal or school resource officer. Inform one other teacher about what you've witnessed.

## 10. Do a security check

Make sure your classroom doors and windows have secure locks. The "two baby boomers" gained entry into their science classroom by slitting an exterior screen door and picking the simple lock with a paper clip.

## 11. Remember the three A's:

**Awareness, alertness and avoidance.** Be aware and alert of your surrounding and avoid putting yourself in situations that can endanger you.

One elementary teacher gave a ride to three middle school students who were hitchhiking . She recognized one of the trio, a student she taught a few years earlier. As they climbed into her back seat, she recalls the conversation with her former student.

"Hello, Jeff. Good to see you again. Don't you remember me? I'm Mrs. Cook your third grade teacher. How are things going with you? Introduce me to your friends."

Her amicable conversation was greeted with blank stares. A few miles down the highway the boys asked to be dropped off. Later she surmised they planned to rob her, but since she recognized one of them, they changed their minds. Never pick up students, even ones you feel you may know.

## 12. Be aware of the flippant remark

Sometimes we ignore an early warning sign such as a flippant remark that makes the class laugh while making us feel extremely uneasy. A conversation with the student is a good idea. The remark needs to be documented, related to our colleagues and to one administrator.

## 13. Report any gang insignias

If you see a gang insignia on a student's notebook, do not confront the student. Instead, talk to your principal, dean or security officer. The student can then be questioned by an administrator without your becoming involved.

## Summary

1. Have a non-published number.
2. Don't identify your mailbox.
3. Buy a mobile phone.
4. When you work late, notify the office.
5. Isolated parking lots are dangerous.
6. Have an emergency school-wide signal.
7. Don't carry open containers into your room.
8. Don't consume unwrapped food.
9. Report suspicious activities.
10. Do a security check.
11. Remember the 3 A's: awareness, alertness and avoidance.
12. Be aware of flippant remarks.
13. Report gang insignias to an administrator.

# 13

## *Lighting Candles In The Darkness*

**I** had just completed an all-day seminar in St. Louis. Collapsing in my airline seat, I buckled up and glanced out the window. The sky was charcoal.

The captain announced we'd be waiting out the bad weather. He was upbeat. The other passengers and I didn't share his enthusiasm. Only 4:00 p.m., yet the sun was completely covered by puffy, black clouds. Winds shook the plane like a sailboat in rough seas.

The plane rocked and rolled for about an hour. The captain came on again with his cheery message: "Since three pilots ahead of us in line for take-off have turned back to the terminal, we're first in line."

Never mind that other pilots had legitimate concerns, never mind that the winds blew with hurricane force, never mind that I envisioned headlines, "Worst Disaster Strikes St. Louis Airport."

I conferred with my seat mate, a woman I hadn't noticed earlier. This didn't seem like such a good idea to us. She offered me chocolate candy. Who cared about calories now?

Lightning splashed patches of white into the darkened cabin. The chipper captain announced we'd be taxiing out. Buckle your seatbelts. We bounced along, hurled by a wind-tide.

I nervously located the exit doors, glanced at the lady beside me, and wondered if we'd survive take-off.

## A Smart Stewardess

The stewardess sensed our trepidation. As we were taxiing down the runway, close to lift-off, she whispered into the microphone: "I think I can, I think I can, I think I can ... " and as soon as we were airborne, she made the sound like a train going up a steep cliff, "Choo-choo, choo-choo, choo-choo."

We laughed. The tension was broken, and we settled comfortably into our seats.

Five minutes later, tornadoes closed the St. Louis airport. It didn't matter. The stewardess' quick wit gave us much needed encouragement and saved the moment.

## The Quick Fix

Encouragement help in conflict situations. Humor relieves tension. Someone once said that giving encouragement is like changing a baby's wet diaper. It doesn't make any permanent changes, but it sure makes us feel better for a while. The following comments came from teachers who participated in my seminars. Their suggestions may help you to brighten a few lives.

# Teachers Light Candles

1. "I tell kids that they'll succeed. They aren't here at Project Pass because they are language deficient, because they 're behavior problems or because they are special education. They're here to PASS."

2. "Even though I teach kids at an alternative middle school, I help them believe that they have an opportunity to make a positive difference in their lives. They can take a bad situation and turn it into a good experience."

3. "Without marking their papers with a grade, I'm writing a response to each writing assignment. It's like writing letters back and forth and the kids are working harder than ever."

4. "Whether they're in my class or not, I greet all children in the hallways."

5. "At least once a week, I ask for personal information — a favorite relative and why. I love my ninth graders and tell them so daily."

6. "I send my students thank you notes."

7. "I give out extra credit 'bucks' for correct answers during class discussion. It encourages my shy students to participate."

8. "By asking one student a day about after-school activities, I've discovered quite a lot about their lives."

9. "I refuse to accept zeroes. I keep students after school to do their work and reward 'no tardies' at the end of the week."

10. "I teach choir. I'm interested in each child as a whole person not just as my personal musical toy. I believe in them and smile before Christmas."

11. "Greeting students at the door, I tell them that we'll have a good a time in class."

Tom Peters said in his book, *In Search Of Excellence*, "Whenever anything happens anywhere, there's a persistent champion involved." The teachers who gave their suggestions for this chapter are all persistent champions.

How do we keep the spark of enthusiasm alive so that we're able to light candles for kids?

# Save the Spark

## 1. Self-Care

Unfortunately, one teacher in Lee County, Florida, lost his hold on reality. Dedicated and devoted special education teacher, Larry Shelton, was described by students and teachers as a quiet, reserved, caring individual. He was frustrated with a system that crowded too many middle school children with special needs into one classroom. He had quit teaching several times, but the 45-year-old Shelton returned twice to Lee County.

One morning after calling in sick for work, he bought a revolver, walked into the administrative building and killed Superintendent John Adams. He then stepped outside and committed suicide. The tragedy is that we lost a good teacher and a great leader.

Personal awareness is our sanity saver and our survival. It prevents us from self-destruction. Someone once said that most people are willing to change, not when they see the light but when they feel the heat. I hope this one section will help you 'feel the heat' and take charge of the circumstances that create your own good mental health.

## 2. The teacher/student relationship

When I was a student in junior high in Miami, I had a wonderful teacher, Mrs. Young. Tall, beautiful even behind brown horn-rim glasses, this red-haired teacher controlled with her Clint Eastwood stare.

Mrs. Young's work went beyond the confines of the classroom. During the last week of May, she helped the eighth grade class plan a Saturday picnic. A tug of war, sack races, a softball game were just some of the highlights, plus all the chips, cokes and grilled hot dogs you could eat.

Two days before the event, I got the mumps and missed the best day in the life of an eighth grader. Three days later, a neighbor girl dropped off a bundle of notes Mrs. Young had inspired my classmates to write to cheer me up.

When Mrs. Young asked our class to write poetry and prose, miracles emerged from our pencils. Toward the end of the year, she published our writings in a ditto blue, stapled edition of "kids stuff" called, *By Us.* I still have the worn copy of the notebook-sized edition of our writings.

Giving a keynote address in a Palm Beach County, 500-seat auditorium, I talked about the power of one teacher's influence. I mentioned Mrs. Young by name. I was a "C" average student, yet she saw some potential in my struggling efforts to write. She didn't tell me "You can't write poetry," so I believed I could.

A hand went up in the back of the room. I said that I'd take questions at the end of the seminar. I continued on about Mrs. Young and how she had given valuable encouragement. The same hand went up and this time I was a little more impatient as I wrapped up my seminar.

Five minutes later the owner of the waving hand stood before me. She wore large, black framed glasses, and her long gray hair was pulled back and tied with a neat bow. The green eyes knew me. She spoke with a familiar husky voice, "Carol," she said, "I'm Mrs. Young." Still my favorite teacher, she's teaching English and inspiring kids in a Miami high school.

The teacher/student relationship never ends because the influence never ends. The relationship between teacher and student is forever.

Immortality isn't reached with all you do, but with all you help others to do. We have to believe in the power of the relationship.

# The Magic Feather

There's a story about a small village school. The drama/music teacher worked on a stage, auditioning children aged seven to ten. They had to sing, act and dance to pass the audition. One little girl gave a good reading and sang well but when she was asked to dance, she looked terrified. "I can't," said the child. The teacher replied, "But of course you can."

Pointing to her hand, the teacher said, "Do you see this feather?" The other kids thought the teacher was crazy because there was no feather. Then the teacher walked over to the child and said, "I'll place 'the feather' in your palm. Now, whatever you do, don't drop the feather." The teacher put on the music and asked the other children to step back and give this child room.

She began moving across the stage, slowly at first, testing the lightness of the feather. She quickly gained confidence, began to dip her body and raised her hand high up in the air, palm up. She turned in circles and finished with a flourish. The scene was magic. The other children gave her a standing ovation. The teacher was able to help the girl unlock the power that was within her. Later, the girl whispered in the teacher's ear, "May I keep the feather?"

When we light candles in the darkness to improve the lives of kids, we are giving the gift of the feather.

## Summary

1. Find creative ways to lift spirits.
2. Create your mental health.
3. Take good care of yourself.
4. Believe in the teacher/student relationship.
5. Give the gift of the feather.

# 14

## *Painless Parent/Teacher* <u>*Conferences*</u>

$T$eaching cannot be done with a closed door. Isolated teachers are poor teachers.

Open the classroom door to the principal, guidance counselor, dean, colleagues and parents who partner with us in creating a golden team that supports children.

### Parents

We tend to view parents as obstacles to learning rather than partners in teaching. They are powerful allies. A parent is the first teacher in a child's life. Parents hold all kinds of keys to kids — car keys, boat keys, skate keys.

Parents usually complain that the only time they hear from school is when there's a problem. Establish early on a positive relationship. Write a back-to-school note, make a phone call or fax a note to the parent's work place.

The first week or two of school, call parents and introduce yourself. Early involvement with parents of special-needs kids can really benefit the child. One teacher who had an ADHD student called home during the first week of school. She asked the parent, "What can we do together to help your son?" Together they devised a strategy that greatly reduced the discipline problems in the classroom.

Parent involvement improves test scores. In a Richmond, Virginia, study performed at an inner city middle school, parents were encouraged to provide a work space at home for their child, praise their child's school work and cooperate with the teacher. The results: twice the grade level gain was made over a group without parental involvement.

When talking with parents, use the following guidelines.

# Conference Don'ts

## 1. Don't say, "I'm sorry to bother you."

Expect the parent to be as concerned, maybe more, than you are. An apology is a negative way to begin any conversation. You aren't selling used cars. You have a right to help this child.

## 2. Don't ask, "How do I handle Janice?"

If you don't know what to do with this child and you're the expert, how do you expect the parent to know how to manage her?

## 3. Don't listen to negative comments.

Negative comments about the student's early school experiences will not be beneficial. Keep your conversation on a positive focus.

# Conferences Do's

## 1. Do project self-confidence.

The parent is nervous, anxious and perhaps angry. Be calm and confident.

## 2. Do say you're interested.

A parent wants a teacher who cares about school and about his/her child.

## 3. Do state your expectations.

"I have your son/daughter's best interest at heart."

"I need you to back me up or your child will lose out."

"I know you did not rear your child to ... "

## 4. Do focus on one issue.

If necessary schedule another conference. Stick to the ten minute time frame and the one issue focus.

## 5. Do call parents early.

"Hello, I'm Mrs. Fuery, your son's second grade teacher. I'd like to make this Robert's best year. What suggestions, comments or concerns do you have?"

# Calling Home

When you have a discipline problem, it is sometimes best to let the student explain his or her behavior to the parent. Dial the home or work number, and hand the phone over to the youngster to report on misbehavior. Coach the student before hand.

Before you dial the number, give the child a chance to say honestly what he/she did.

Ask the student, "What did you do first, second and then what happened?"

One high school student came into the classroom singing a popular song with the lyrics, "My love is as hard as a rock." He sang off-key but his editing of the lyrics to "hard as my c---," got him into trouble. The teacher dialed the mother's work number. It was an embarrassed and apologetic young man telling his parents the new version of the lyrics.

If getting the correct phone number is difficult, consider what an assistant principal in rural Texas said to a reluctant student, "You have no choice. Give me your number. I've got a boat, a horse and a four-wheel drive jeep. I'll get to your house one way or the other." She laughed when she said, "My students knew I was just crazy enough to do it, too."

## Irate Parent Conference

One teacher commented, "Meeting the parents helps me forgive their children."

You have seen the sign, perhaps on your campus, "All unauthorized persons please report to the office immediately." Schools aren't always user friendly toward parents. Your understanding of the parent's anger will help keep you calm, cool and confident.

## Understand Parents

An upset, irate parent is the norm at parent/teacher conferences. Realize that much of the anger is the outer reflection of parents love for the child. Try

**151**

not to take the parent's anger as an attack on your worth as a teacher. The parent's anger may be a trigger for the frustration and unhappiness felt while in school.

## 1. Invite into your space

Introduce yourself. Shake the parent's hand. Don't call parent by his or her first name unless asked to do so. Say, "Thank you, Mr. or Mrs. Parent for coming. Would you be comfortable sitting here?"

Be sure that the parent sits down immediately. We have the most resistance while standing. Seat them preferably away from your desk. Arrange chairs at same eye level and close enough together to convey warmth.

## 2. Offer comfort

Offer a cup of coffee, a soft drink or glass of water. Even if you don't want the beverage, get yourself a cup of coffee. Why? You will use this as a prop. When you need to slow the conversation down, pause to sip the coffee. It will give you valuable thinking time.

Let the parents know from the beginning that you love their child as if he or she were your own. Say, "I know that I'm not perfect and that I have things to learn. I'm eager to learn from you.

## 3. Say, "We have a problem ... "

Then let the parent vent. (Use the reflective listening guidelines in Chapter Nine.) Give eye contact. Paraphrase or simply restate the parents comments and concerns. Use appropriate facial concerns. Use appropriate facial expressions and body language to show your sincere interest.

## 4. State the problem

Begin by re-stating the problems that you can both agree on. This establishes you and the parent as a powerful team. You might use phrases like: "In my personal experience, I've found this to be true? Do you agree?" At this point the parent is nodding his/her head and agreeing with you.

## 5. Offer documentation

This step may or may not be necessary. If you need it, use the form for documentation at end of this chapter. This can include a list of grades, homework papers, tests, etc.

## 6. Decide on a follow up

At this point, you and the parent are partners trying to do what is best for the child. Say, "Since we share this problem, 'What's the best thing for me to do?' "

"How can you help at home?"

"What will the student do?"

## 7. Touch base — communicate

Say, "What works best — a phone call at work, leaving a message on your answering machine, a note home with the student, a fax to your place of business?"

## 8. Closure

Shake the parent's hand and use his/her name. Thank parent for coming. Tell the parent you have another appointment.

Remember that while the parent is talking, it is rude to rise from your chair. While you're talking, is the appropriate time to stand. End with a positive, closing statement. Use the parent's name. "Thank you for meeting with me, Mr./Ms. Parent. I appreciate your valuable time, and I know we can work this out."

# Win Parents

1. Call early in the school year.
2. Ask if child has special learning needs.
3. Send home the discipline policy.
4. Arrange incentives for Back-to-School Night.

# Letter Home

Send after first two to three weeks of school (perfect for two days before Open House)

A student earns the following letter, if he/she has all work turned in and has completed a grade of "C" or better.

---

September

Dear Parent or Guardian,

This is a friendly note to inform you that your "young person" _____ has all assignments and other work in. I'm proud of this student's efforts because it takes self-discipline and a caring attitude to keep up in our classroom. So many times we teachers send notes home when there are deficiencies, and not when there is something to praise.

There is a saying, "Catch them doing something good," circulating among our schools. I have looked for the good, and I have found it in _____. With encouragement this success will continue.

Sincerely,

---

**Parent/Teacher Conference
Target Sheet**

Teacher_____ Date_____

Student_____

Parent's names_____

Home phone_____ Work_____


Problem summary_____

Suggested solution_____

Signatures_____

# Summary

1. **Contact parents early.**
2. **Use Target Sheets for documentation.**
3. **Send good letters home.**

# 15

## *Salvage Your* *<u>Self-Esteem</u>*

When a friend of mine, Steve was in college, he asked a girl for a tennis date. She accepted, but told him after their first set, "It's not a date unless you feed me."

I like this young woman's philosophy. Sharing and feeding should be part of a new friendship or a healthy relationship. But what about the teacher who fills empty spirits and nurtures students every day? Who feeds the teacher?

### An Empty Spirit

I was invited to speak in a rural school district outside of Phoenix, Arizona. When the superintendent called, he explained that a year earlier the mining company, this small town's major employer, had closed. Because his teachers started school with uncertain futures, he asked me to give them a boost.

The morning of my session, I awoke early and took a walk through the desert. The scenery was unbelievable. Majestic, towering green cacti were offset by a deep blue, almost purple sky. A few pink clouds were close to the horizon and surreal. I was captivated by the power and aura of the setting.

The superintendent met me and we drove into the early morning sunlight. When I saw the downtown area, my heart sank. Once-thriving stores were boarded up. The deserted main street was full of potholes. What was once a bustling village was now a ghost town.

We pulled next to a low-roofed set of red brick buildings. I was to speak in the small unairconditioned cafeteria. It was 90 degrees at 9 a.m. But the heat was not as troublesome as the low energy. The teachers were dazed and lethargic. Hot coffee and sweet rolls didn't help.

After about 20 minutes of my seminar, I realized everyone paid close attention, but the energy was missing. I attempted a few anecdotes which usually bring laughter — nothing. The room was as dead as a morgue. Someone once said, "You can dress up the corpse, but you can't give it life." My usual high energy faltered.

My main goal was to get the seminar over and catch my flight back to Florida. As a last resort, I ended the morning with a review activity. The participants who at this point sat silent, were to stand one at a time, speak into a microphone and express what they had learned or re-learned. All participated, even principals and the superintendent. Moved and encouraged by my words, they gave responses that amazed me. Their voices were a testimony to hope.

# Opportunities

We miss opportunities to be encouraging to ourselves, our colleagues and our students.

Teaching kids on an empty spirit leads to failure. A female colleague, who had filed for divorce from the husband she still loved, described her feelings this way, "Some days I could barely lift my head from the desk. How could I help my fifth graders when I couldn't even help myself? No wonder my year was a disaster."

When we teach on an empty spirit, we give what we don't have. The better way is to nurture and care for ourselves. When we have high self-esteem, we take care of ourselves. We teach on a full heart.

## Salvage Your Self-Esteem

Dr. Nathaniel Branden's book, *How To Raise Your Self-Esteem*, defines self-esteem as "the confidence in our right to be happy, feel worthy, deserving and entitled to assert our needs and wants." The following suggestions salvage our self-esteem.

### 1. Create alone time

Time alone is a great healer. Ding Darling was a cartoonist and conservationist in the 30's and 40's. He visited and fell in love with Captiva on Florida's west coast and returned many winters to draw. He owned a rustic, piling house that edged a mangrove bay. When he wanted to concentrate on his work, he raised a drawbridge kept away unwanted visitors.

Every teacher needs a drawbridge. Renewing your energy means completely dropping your classroom cares and concentrating on whatever pleases you at the moment. You need time away from the fray.

Creative solutions to problems don't grow in the midst of battle. They grow in the quiet moments of solitude and peace that we give ourselves. No one can grant us alone time but ourselves.

We need the freedom to be alone. We make time for returning phone calls, for exercise, for church. We need to make time for ourselves.

Sometimes we silence the persistent voice inside us that tells us we're crowding too many events into too little space. When it becomes necessary to shut the world out, grant yourself permission to pull up a drawbridge. How do you do this?

## 2. Set appropriate boundaries

Getting the time we desperately need and deserve means setting a boundary. The most important thing to remember is that we can't set a boundary when we consider the other person's feelings. We must consider our needs first.

It's the human condition to constantly test boundaries. My neighbor, Richard, has two small children, ages three and five. His children ride their tricycles in the driveway. A red line painted on the concrete sets their safe distance from the road. The youngsters know they aren't allowed past his line, yet his oldest daughter rides beyond it by a few inches. One day as I watched his little girl, he commented that he purposely left the line a good two feet from the road, knowing full well his children would go beyond it, testing the boundary.

When writing this book, I told my friends and family that I can't be reached from 8 a.m. to 12 p.m., every day. Yet, I still have friends who call during my writing hours or worse yet, drop by my office unannounced. My drawbridge is an answering machine and a locked door.

### 3. Plan a meditation moment

More than a 25 years after Maharishi Mahesh Yogi introduced Transcendental Meditation to America. Meditation has gone mainstream. Relaxation techniques help us calm down, focus on our teaching and solve minor health problems.

### 4. Trust your instincts

A friend of mine is president of an international company. He says about his top executives, "I won't hire a man or a woman who can't trust his/her instincts. Many times it's next to impossible to get all the facts. By the time you have all the answers, it's too late to act. You have to trust your instincts."

Our instincts are those little voices inside us. They help us survive. By creating a few moments for meditation, we allow that valuable subconscious information to enter our conscious thought.

### 5. Mental compartments

I separate my school and home life. It helps that I live on an island in Florida and cross several bridges and a causeway before I get home. When I cross the first bridge, I leave problems and troubles behind me. I know that tomorrow is another day. That is creating a mental compartment.

People working in the helping professions need to detach concern. Mother Theresa was asked, "You work with the sick and dying children all the time. How can you stand it?" She answered, "We love them while they are here. When they leave or die, we let them go."

My friends in Miami, Florida's inner city schools tell of kids who love the security of school so much they need to be chased off campus by 5 p.m. They'd rather be at school. But we can't care, worry or concern ourselves with students 24 hours a day. We'd lose our effectiveness and our sanity. "Loving them while they are here" is the answer.

## Summary

1. **Create alone time.**
2. **Set appropriate boundaries.**
3. **Plan a meditation moment.**
4. **Trust your instincts.**
5. **Mental compartments.**

# 16

# _The Courageous Teacher_

"It's too bad when you go to work and you don't love it, especially in our profession. If you don't get excited every morning about getting into that room with all those kids with their bright eyes waiting for you ... then get the hell out of education."

Leo Buscaglia, Author

## A Buddhist Fable

One of my favorite stories is a Buddhist fable written 2,000 years ago about a beautiful young elephant that lived in the forest near Benares. According to the legend, the elephant was as white as crane's down, and her size and strength were so great that the men who captured her gave her as a present to the king.

The king entrusted her to the elephant trainers to be taught to stand firm and to follow commands, but the trainers were harsh with her and beat her with their elephant goads. One day, maddened by pain, she broke free of them and escaped.

The elephant ran as fast as she could for many days, traveling far into the Himalayan Mountains. She outdistanced all the king's men who were chasing her, and in time they all went home and she was free.

But the elephant still raced on, and although time passed she did not reduce her pace, or forget for a moment that she had once been a captive. Every time a twig snapped or a breath of wind rustled the trees, she dashed off at full speed, thrashing her trunk wildly from side to side.

Finally a compassionate tree sprite could stand the elephant's pain no longer. The sprite leaned out of a fork in a tree one day and whispered into the elephant's ear, "Do you fear the wind? It only moves the clouds and dries the dew. You ought to look into your mind. It's fear that has captured you."

And the minute the wood sprite had spoken, the beautiful elephant realized that she had nothing to fear but the habit of being afraid, and she began to enjoy life again.

## Teaching Takes Courage

Teaching school takes courage often more than we think we possess and more than we think we should need. It is easy to have courage when colleagues applaud our efforts and much more difficult to fight the status quo.

Know that our courage expands with use. Be brave. Do what's in the child's best interest. Fear prevents us from growing, changing and chancing. We are braver than we think. Teachers with the most confidence aren't waiting around for students to validate them. They validate themselves.

# Victim or Prizefighter?

There are really only two ways to approach teaching — as a victim or a gallant prizefighter. I was invited to do a before-the-school-year keynote address for the Silsbee Independent School District in Silsbee, Texas. That's where I met the legendary, Mr. Lindsey, a teacher beginning his 50th year in the classroom.

When I first heard about him, I imagined a small, decrepit man shuffling to school. I met Bevil Lindsey in the back of the crowded auditorium, sitting between two young and attractive female teachers. Mr. Lindsey was tall, lean and handsome with a strong, energetic voice and a wonderful smile.

His principal, Fred Miller, told me a few things about Bevil, who started teaching when he was 20 years old. The students at Laura-Reeves Elementary School ask to be on Mr. Lindsey's hall. He gets to school early, and before class has a morning study hall to help kids with their homework. The parents have a two-year waiting list to get their children into his classroom. I interviewed Mr. Lindsey and was fascinated by his enthusiasm.

"I love learning. Learning is contagious like your laughter and your personality.

"I like making students think learning is fun. I've tried everything in my tenure — 50 years — it's almost obscene. My students ask me if I ever feel bad and I tell them that when I feel bad, that's when I smile the most. The kids say you must feel bad all the time.

"Inclusion and main-streaming are just new terms for an old idea. When I taught in the 1940's I taught sixth, seventh and eighth grade all in one room. I used all the learning styles as I do now — visual, auditory,

**165**

kinesthetic. I can teach 50 in a classroom as well as I can teach two. I believe in a controlled classroom. I want their attention, all of them. I keep them together as a group, and I tie-in what I teach to their home lives.

"When a student asks a question that I know could be answered if the material were read, I use humor to get my point across. I sing out, 'You didn't read it.' And the class laughs, even the student who asked the question. And student will admit, 'You are right. I did not read it.'

"I teach children on all levels. I get folders (from the exceptional education teachers) and I hate to look at them. Before I read the folders, I don't know who is main-streamed and who isn't. The first week of school, I have six kids from special education classes and four of them made 100 on the physics test."

"I introduce my kids to physics and they just love it. They don't want to leave class. They fuss when the bell rings." Bevil Lindsey

## Making Changes

There is a little bit of Mr. Lindsay in all prizefighters. He continues: "Good teachers are flexible. They constantly change and try new ideas. I mix the new ideas with the old ideas and discover what works best with kids."

Try new ideas. Make changes. Remember that deciding to make a change and changing are two different things. If there are three frogs on a log, and one decides to jump, how many frogs are on the log?

Three. Deciding to jump isn't jumping. Teachers who are brave warriors, jump.

Change makes you vulnerable. What could possibly be more chancy than standing before a group of kids everyday, trying something brand new? Good teachers have courage.

There are moments when we have to know in our hearts, "I am a good teacher. I am a worthwhile person. I am as important to other human beings as they are to me."

To survive in the new teaching environment, you must exercise the ingenuity and boldness of a veteran warrior. Besides a prizefighter, you must be a daring guerrilla on patrol.

Be the intrepid warrior on the front line of change.

Acknowledge your power and the incredible opportunity to open doors for and with children. The wise use of that power drives you, refuels you and keeps you young.

"Teaching school is unfinished business. Unlike a real estate agent or a builder, teachers work in great doubt. We don't have a finished product. Our students are works in progress. Yet, somehow I always felt I made a difference."

Ruth Rigby, Golden Apple Teacher,
Lee County, Florida

Bevil Lindsay put it this way: "I feel like I've been a successful person. I hear from my former students from all over this country. I was in Houston at a convention in a room full of people and someone shouted from across the room, 'There's the man who was my inspiration.' Everyone stopped talking and stared. The woman was pointing directly at me. Her name was Tara Collins. I taught her in the seventh grade. Everywhere I go I meet someone I taught. I can't escape."

Inspirational teachers don't escape. Because to be a child in Mrs. Rigby's class or Mr. Lindsay's class or in your class, is to be your child forever.

## *About the Author*

If you liked this book, then you'll love Carol Fuery's seminars. She is a motivator. Her delightful sense of humor is a breath of fresh air in a classroom gone stale.

Carol Fuery is one of the most sought after speakers and trainers on motivation, self-esteem and discipline. She has inspired audiences throughout North America with her expertise and her ability to address difficult topics with energy, insight and astounding clarity.

Her seminars range from a keynote kicking-off the school year to a full-day workshop breaking up mid-term blues. Author of four self-help books for educators, Carol Fuery's workshops are packed with humorous anecdotes from her 27 years of solid educational experience.

For further information on her training and seminars, please write or call:

Carol Fuery Seminars
P.O. Box 461
Captiva, FL  33924
(941) 472-3459

## *Share Your Feedback*

Send us your comments and concerns about *Discipline Strategies.*

If you have used a strategy from this book, send us a photo or write us a letter describing what you achieved; how it affected your students; what types of things you observed in student behavior, interest and skill level.

Be sure to include your name, grade level, school, school phone number, fax number, and your expressed permission for us to reprint your idea.

Please do not call. We evaluate each activity and respond only to those activities considered for inclusion in a forthcoming publication.

If you want your materials returned, please include a stamped self-addressed envelope. Write/fax your ideas to the address below.

Sanibel SandDollar Publications, Inc.
P.O. Box 461
Captiva, FL 33924
Fax: (941) 472-0699

## To Order Books by Carol Fuery:

- ☐ **Discipline Strategies** .................. $15.95
- ☐ **Winning Year One** .................. $13.95
- ☐ **Successful Subbing** .................. $11.95
- ☐ **Are You Still Teaching?** ................ $15.95
- ☐ **Order the set (includes shipping)** ........ $55.00
  *Florida residents add 6% sales tax.*
- ☐ **Yes! Please rush me your free seminar packet.**

*Shipping $5 for first book, $1 for each additional book*
*Personal Checks and Purchase Orders*
*gladly accepted. No Credit Cards.*

---

**PHONE-IN YOUR ORDER**
Toll Free Call: (800)330-3459 or (941) 472-3459
**FAX US YOUR ORDER**
Or Purchase Order to: (941) 472-0699
**MAIL ORDER FORM TO:**
Sanibel SandDollar Publications, Inc.
Box 461, Captiva, Florida 33924

---

**FULL REFUND GUARANTEE**
*If for any reason, you are not satisfied, return*
*books for a full refund. Any time. No hassles.*

✂····································································

Name:_____

Job Title:_____

School or County Name:_____

Mailing Address:_____

City:_____ St:___ Zip:_____

Phone:_____ Fax:_____

Purchase Order #_____

## To Order Books by Carol Fuery:

- ☐ **Discipline Strategies** .................... $15.95
- ☐ **Winning Year One** .................... $13.95
- ☐ **Successful Subbing** .................... $11.95
- ☐ **Are You Still Teaching?** ................ $15.95
- ☐ **Order the set (includes shipping)** ........ $55.00
  *Florida residents add 6% sales tax.*
- ☐ **Yes! Please rush me your free seminar packet.**

*Shipping $5 for first book, $1 for each additional book*
*Personal Checks and Purchase Orders*
*gladly accepted. No Credit Cards.*

---

**PHONE-IN YOUR ORDER**
Toll Free Call: (800)330-3459 or (941) 472-3459
**FAX US YOUR ORDER**
Or Purchase Order to: (941) 472-0699
**MAIL ORDER FORM TO:**
Sanibel SandDollar Publications, Inc.
Box 461, Captiva, Florida 33924

---

**FULL REFUND GUARANTEE**
*If for any reason, you are not satisfied, return*
*books for a full refund. Any time. No hassles.*

✂ ·······································································································

Name:_____

Job Title:_____

School or County Name:_____

Mailing Address:_____

City:_____ St:____ Zip:_____

Phone:_____ Fax:_____

Purchase Order #_____